THE FAUVES

Author: Nathalia Brodskaïa

Layout:
Baseline Co. Ltd,
District 3, Ho Chi Minh City
Vietnam

ISBN: 978-1-68325-940-4

Printed in

Nathalia Brodskaïa

THE FAUVES

Rewriting the Rules of Colour and Freedom

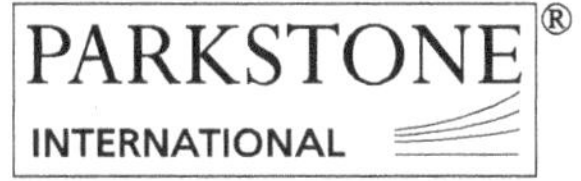

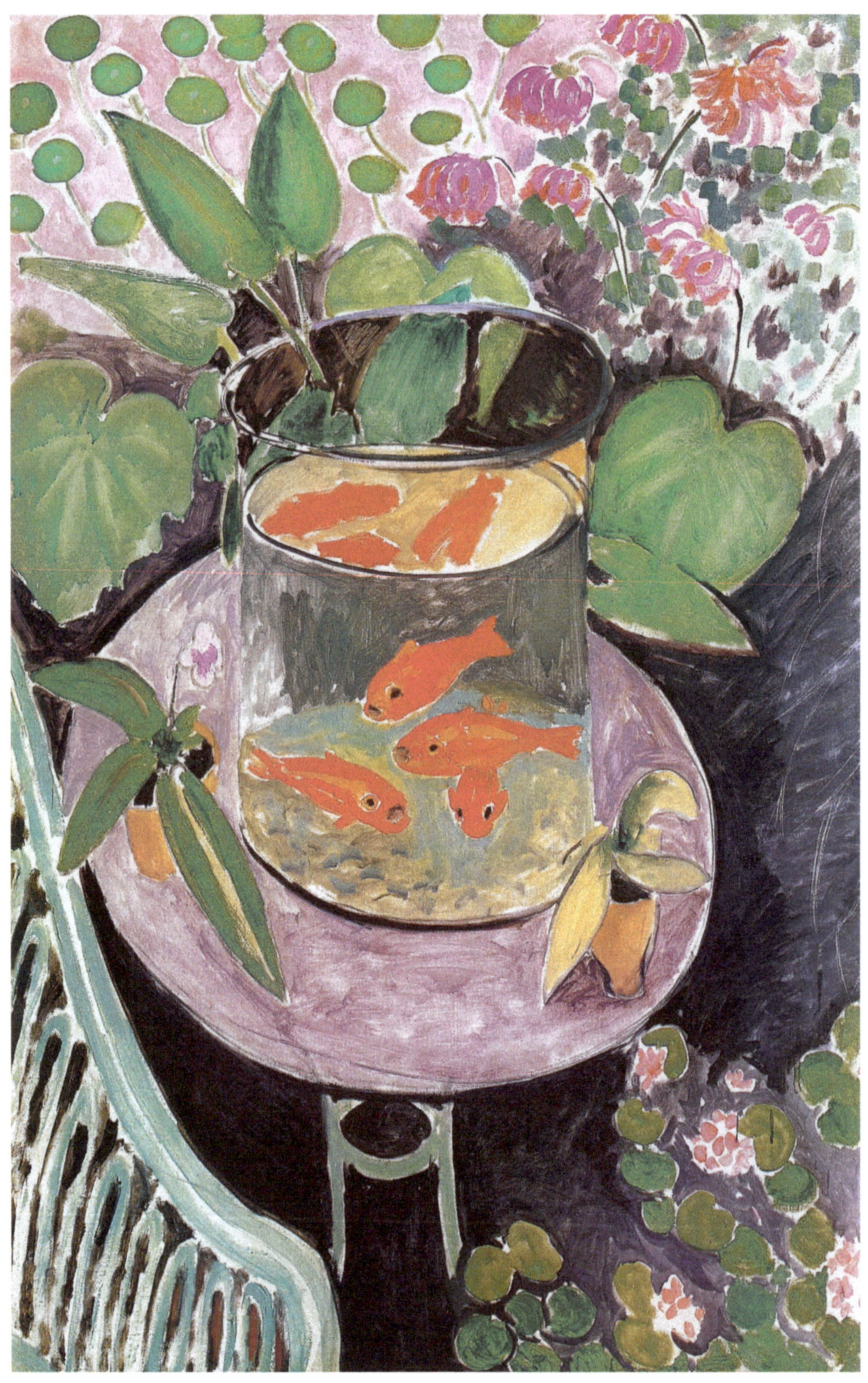

CONTENTS

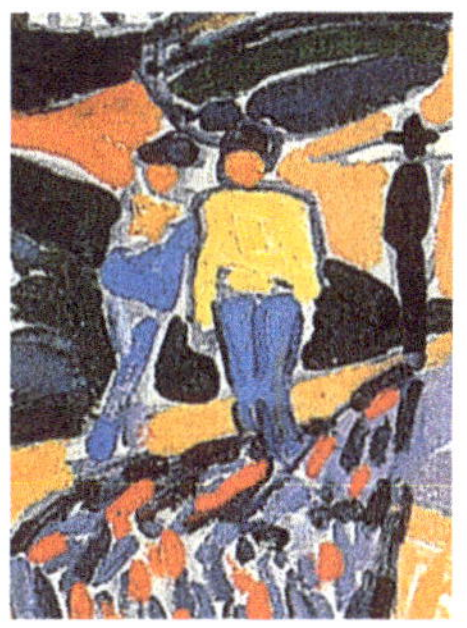

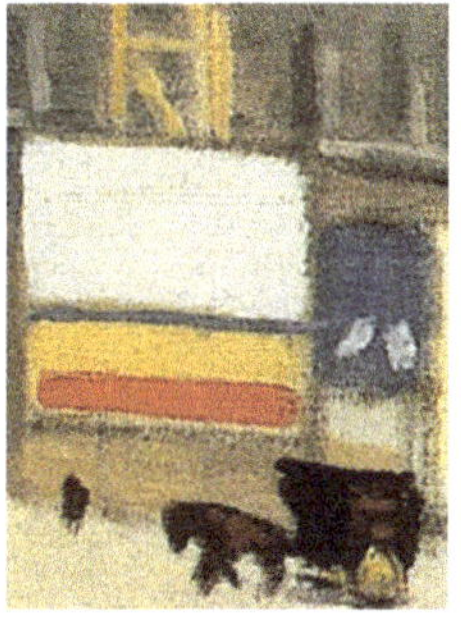

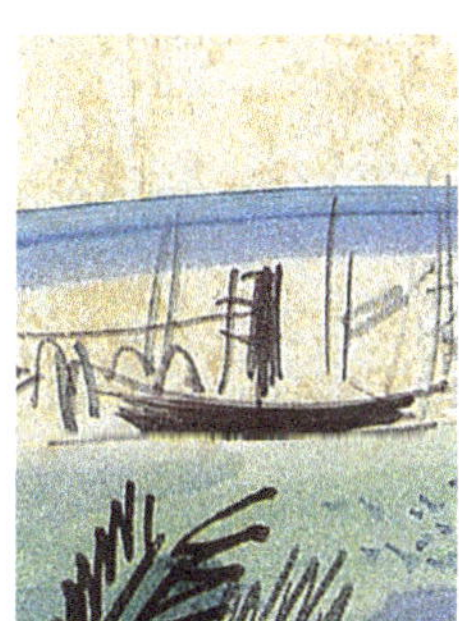

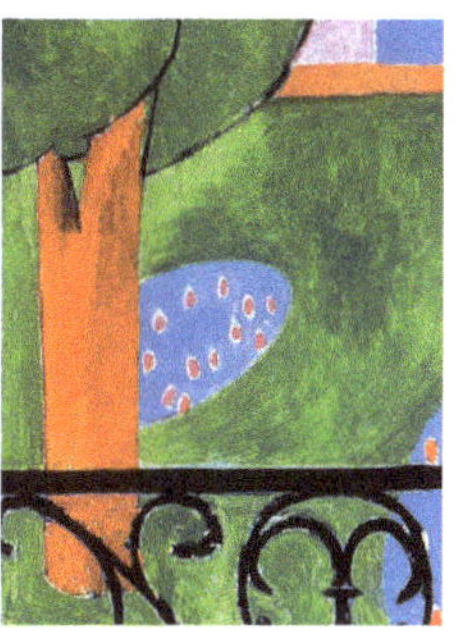

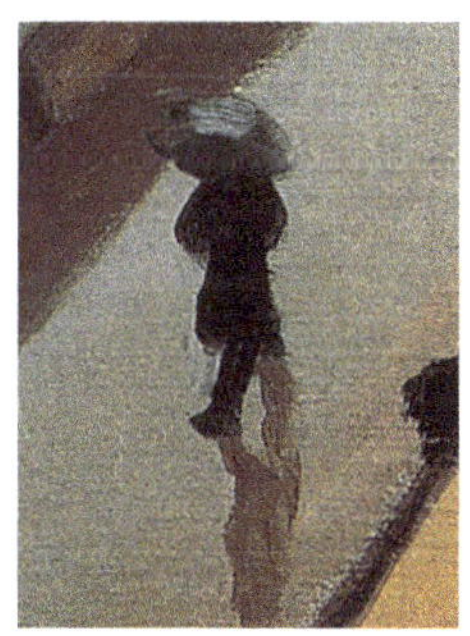

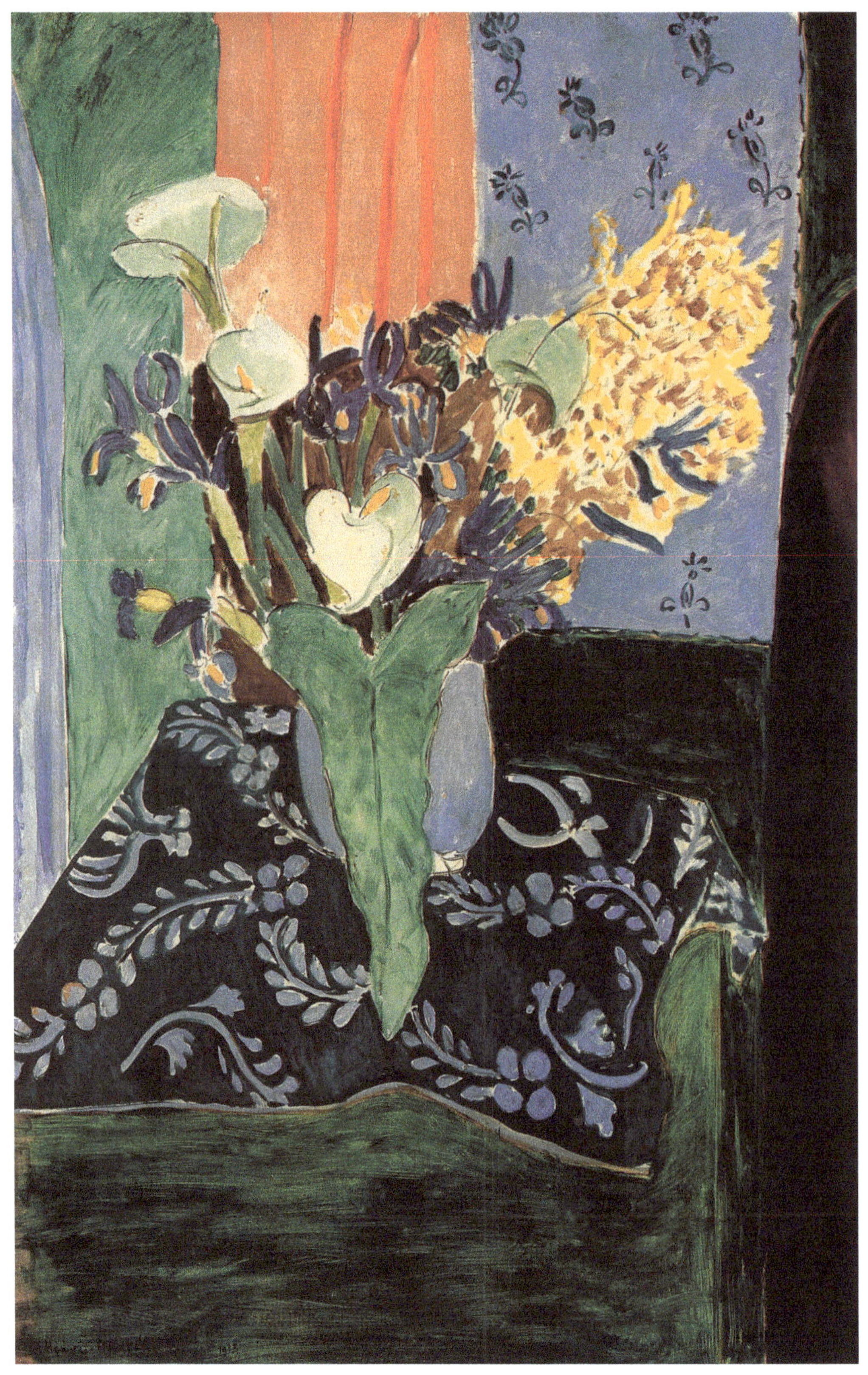

A HISTORY OF FAUVISM

Decade follows decade in art, like waves breaking on a beach, each bringing its own "deposits" which, in turn, cover those that came before, dimming what had once seemed strikingly brilliant. But time does not work on everything with equal force. The art of the Fauves has not faded. Born within French painting at the turn of the century, Fauvism immediately demanded attention.

The stormy reaction it provoked on its emergence in Paris in 1905 was, in itself, an acknowledgement of the strength of this new phenomenon in the fine arts. Fauvism was a real danger to academically congealed art calculated to appeal to the narrow-minded customer, to all painting which sought after prosperity by carefully absorbing innovation, turning it into the fashionable that would shock no-one through unwarranted boldness.

▲ **Henri Matisse**,
Goldfish, 1911.
Oil on canvas, 147 x 98 cm.
Pushkin Museum of Fine Arts, Moscow. (p. 4)

◄ **Henri Matisse**,
Calla Lilies, Irises and Mimosas, 1913.
Oil on canvas, 145.5 x 97 cm.
Pushkin State Museum of Fine Arts, Moscow.

Two or three years proved sufficient for the Fauvist painters to acquire – if not a permanent public, then at least their own dealers and admirers. The hostile voices which continued to make themselves heard were not enough to hinder the Fauves from competing freely with other trends. Each of them lived a life in keeping with his character and the unique features of his work, yet none of them experienced long years of hopeless poverty or a sense of impotence in the struggle with the might of official art. None of the Fauves left a studio full of works piled up and never sold – in this sense fate was kinder to them than to Gauguin, Van Gogh, or Toulouse-Lautrec. Even during their lifetimes, the Fauves' paintings had found a place in the greatest private collections and then in museums, while they themselves were written about in the press and respected by contemporaries.

The Fauves were acknowledged masters before they reached the age when grey locks and a noble bearing often stood substitute for true measures of talent. It might seem that when the general public would become more familiar with them, the intensity of the first reaction would diminish, but this was not the case. They are all long since gone, yet one still experiences a sense of shock on encountering their paintings.

Fauvism received its name in 1905. In October of that year, a number of young painters – about ten altogether – presented their works at the 'Salon d'Automne ' in Paris. Their unusually bright works vibrant with colour were assembled in a single hall. In his account of the exhibition for the 27 October edition of the magazine Gil Blas, critic Louis Vauxcelles wrote: "In the centre of Room VII stands a child's torso by Albert Marquet. The candour of this bust is striking in the midst of an orgy of pure colour: Donatello among the wild beasts." This unexpected description from the pen of an art expert – "wild beasts," fauves – proved so apt that within just a few days it was taken up by the press, its originator forgotten, and began a life of its own. A simple explanation, then, in which chance played a significant role, and from that moment on, the names of Matisse, Derain, Vlaminck, Van Dongen, Camoin, Puy, Marquet, Manguin, Rouault, Dufy, Friesz, Valtat and a few others were generally associated with the word Fauvism.

The very way in which the term originated is positive proof that the phenomenon it described already possessed definite recognizable characteristics. Nobody at that time, including Vauxcelles himself, was able to indicate its boundaries or predict the full Henri Matisse, significance of what had emerged. Most likely, the fact that interest in Fauvism has remained keen for more than three quarters of a century causes us to reflect again on what essentially occurred at the 'Salon d'Automne ' and who it was that Vauxcelles christened "wild beasts."

In the second half of the twentieth century, reminiscences about the Fauves and the assessments of contemporaries inevitably gave way to the research of art historians, yet this process revealed a surprising quality of Fauvism: even with the test of time, it remains as hard as ever to define precisely its chronology and characteristics which defy consistent classification. It is no coincidence that, from the middle of the century on, one exhibition has followed another as testimony that interest in Fauvism now extends beyond Paris, beyond even Europe. Fauvism is linked to other artistic phenomena of the same period, while, time and again, scholars return to the assembly of canvases with which it all began in 1905. The reasons for this attention lie, most probably above all, in two obvious facts: with the passage of time, new aspects of the revolution which took place in painting at the beginning of the century are being discovered and, no less important, the "young wild beasts" of the opening years of the century all, without exception, became major figures in French twentieth-century painting. Cause enough to carry out one more examination of Fauvism as a conglomeration of unquestionable individual artistic talents and as an artistic association, which brought about not the levelling of talents but, on the contrary, the development of each of the artists' own creative strengths.

For the outside observer, the background in Paris was still undoubtedly formed by the exhibitions of the official Salons, both by virtue of the great quantity of works presented at them, the large number of participants, and because of the predominant interest of the critics in them and their influence on

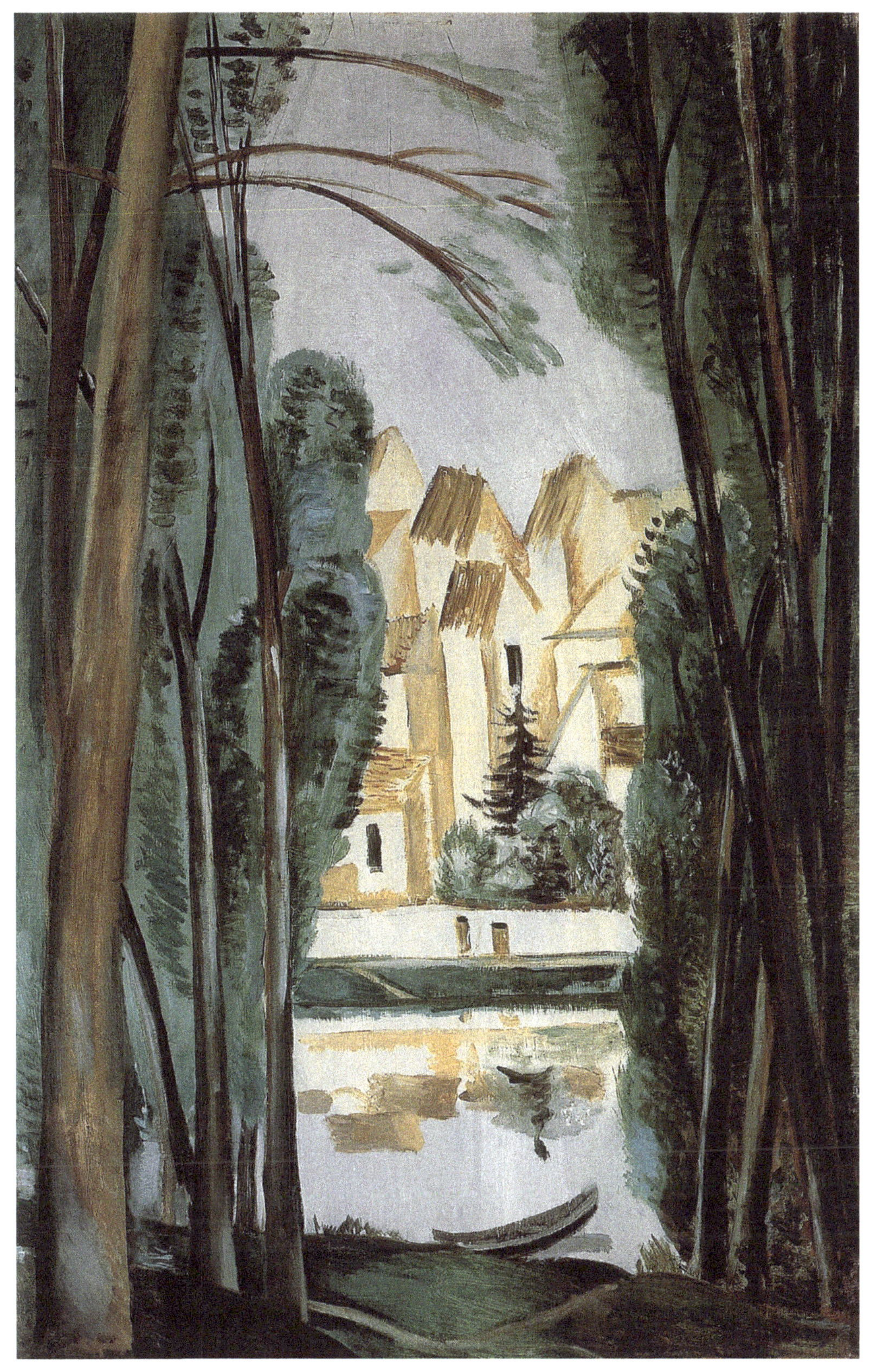

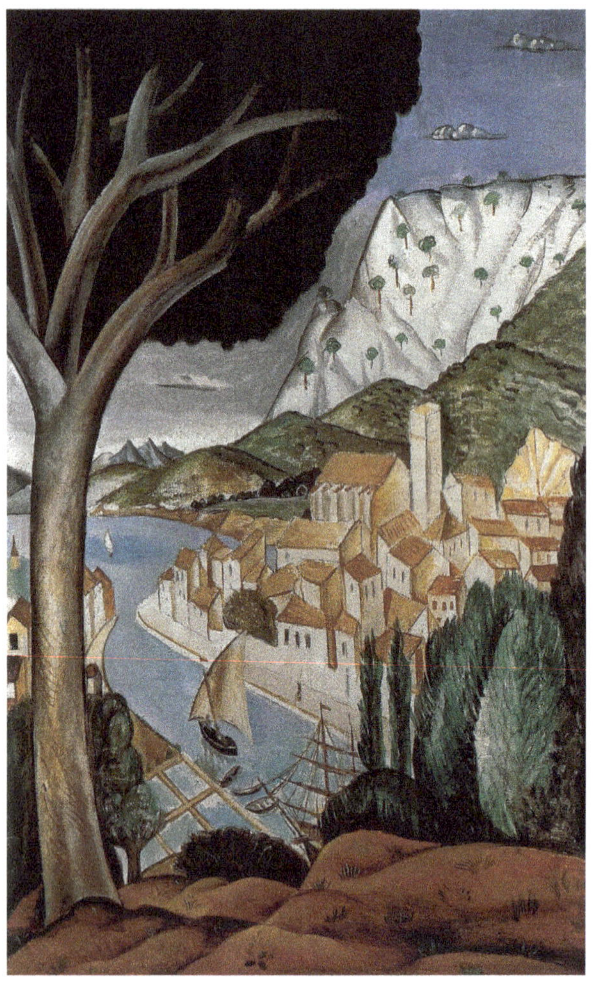

▲ **André Derain,**
Landscape with a Boat by the Bank, c. 1915.
Oil on canvas, 100 x 65 cm.
State Hermitage Museum, Saint Petersburg. (p. 9)

▲ **André Derain,**
Martigues (Harbour in Provence), 1913.
Oil on canvas, 141 x 90 cm.
State Hermitage Museum, Saint Petersburg.

the art market. This situation endured right up until the end of the nineteenth century and it seemed that nothing, even in the future, would be powerful enough to shake this stronghold of the Academy. It is enough to recall how many of the Impressionists, who were opposed on principle to academic art, nevertheless, dreamt of getting into the Salon since that meant hope, if not of being bought, then at least of becoming known to a certain extent within the circle of potential patrons.

The situation changed somewhat in the final years of the century. An even greater number of artists were working outside the circle of the Salon. By the beginning of the twentieth century, earning a living was no longer directly linked to success at the Salons for the younger generation of artists. New art found its own dealers who acted as middlemen between buyers and artists. It is not possible, then, to say that at the time of the Fauves' appearance, the Salons were still what they had been, although the changes that had taken place did not markedly affect their art. By this time, though, the grandeur verging on megalomania of the Salons, coupled with the conservative academic style, was often regarded with unconcealed irony.

Even the Impressionists – men of the recent past, although by now they were one by one going to their graves – and the peaceful artists of the Nabis group who had not involved themselves in the struggle (Edouard Vuillard, Pierre Bonnard, Maurice Denis, and the others) found themselves in a position of resistance, yet could not discover another place to exhibit besides the often derided 'Salon des Indépendants'.

By 1905, the 'Salon des Indépendants 'already had a history of its own. It had been founded in 1884 by artists rejected by the official Salon and was an exhibition which opened its doors to all the aggrieved without exception, promoting the principle of equality by not having a jury or awards. The established critics devoted much effort to creating a reputation for the 'Salon des Indépendants 'as they did acquiring a fantastic assemblage of works by certain cranks which might be visited so as to amuse oneself at the naive paintings of Douanier Rousseau and others like him.

Yet the impenetrable conservatism of the official exhibitions was of unexpected service to the 'Salon des Indépendants': by the early twentieth century the latter's emphatic objectivity, equally hospitable to all, had given way to a quite definite tendency. The path taken by this association of artists led to their 'Salon des Indépendants 'becoming a bastion of new trends; even the Impressionists found themselves no more welcome there than at the official exhibitions. However, at the moment, the fate of the Impressionists is not our concern. They could no longer be numbered among the ranks of the rejected while the younger generation badly needed an opportunity to demonstrate their art and to have some sort of association to stand up in defence of it, even if that association was still without a definite aim or programme.

In the early years of the twentieth century it was no longer possible to overlook the Salon des Indépendants. Even the lumbering state machinery was obliged, if not to reckon with it in the full sense of the word, then at least to make a gesture in its direction. Even earlier, the Direction des Beaux-Arts had sent its commissioners to the 'Salon des Indépendants 'to select pieces for purchase by the state, but they had never once found anything suitable. In 1902 the commissioner was Léonce Bénédit, curator of the Musée du Luxembourg, but he, too, found it possible to acquire only some "très delicates" sketches by Édouard Vuillard. Yet the choice at the 1902 'Salon des Indépendants 'was a fairly wide one. Among the many others, there were almost forty works by five of the future Fauves led by Henri Matisse, and an attentive eye would have discovered them the year before as well.

However, they were probably not yet perceived as a distinct phenomenon or even as an association, more so since they themselves did not make an aim of exhibiting together. In 1902 they failed not only to disturb anyone, but even to attract any great attention at all. The 'Salon des Indépendants 'was then simply one of the possible places for showing their work – a few of the future Fauves managed to get a work or two into the official Salon de la Société Nationale des Beaux-Arts (Van Dongen, Manguin) or even into the International Exhibition held in Venice (Dufy, Friesz, Rouault). The nascent Fauves had not been noticed due to the fact that they were still outsiders, even for the 'Salon des Indépendants 'where in the course of time they would establish their own authority and preferences.

For the future Fauves, however, these first public appearances, for all their failure to create an impression, did play a major role: a process of formation was underway, formation not simply of their grouping, but of their artistic outlook. Their complex, yet definite conception of their own painting, three years later would attain not only perceptible form, but also recognition. On 31 October, in the Petit Palais, a new exhibition opened which had not previously existed – the 'Salon d'Automne '. Also founded by painters who had been rejected by the official salons, this exhibition was, at the moment of its creation, a strange combination of the most progressive forces in art and others which were quite conservative by the standards of the time. In contrast to the Salon des Indépendants, here there was a jury, selected five days before the exhibition. The deputy chief curator of the Petit Palais, Yvanhoé Rambosson, managed to secure premises for the new salon in the basements of his museum. From the very onset, the exhibition committee included a number of Moreau's former pupils – Georges Desvallières, Henri Matisse, Albert Marquet and Georges Rouault. In 1903 only four of the future Fauves exhibited here – Matisse, Marquet, Rouault and Manguin; however, these artists not only took advantage of a new opportunity to exhibit, but at once began to look on the 'Salon d'Automne ' as the main venue for presenting their work. In contrast to the already customary Salon des Indépendants, the 'Salon d'Automne ' attracted both visitors and critics through its intriguing novelty. So it became their principal exhibition place and this was the start of a new era in their lives.

The Salon des Indépendants, which opened on 24 March 1905, can be reckoned the first real display of Fauvist painting as a fully-formed phenomenon and was truly triumphal: one hundred works by fourteen artists, each of whom became a prominent figure in Fauvist painting!

The group had grown in size by comparison with the previous year and the two new members who joined not only intensified the radiance of what already existed, but also injected some brilliant and original talent into it. After a century has gone by, it is hard to imagine whether without them the group of Fauves could have produced the bombshell in European art that was their emergence in 1905. The two figures in question are André Derain and Maurice de Vlaminck, two friends from the Paris suburb of Chatou who had become acquainted with Matisse as early as 1901 but had never before exhibited with him. Despite all that has been said, the Fauves were not recognized as a group in the spring of 1905. Naturally, the critic Roger-Marx cited the names of many of them together with highly sympathetic appraisals of their painting, showing respect for free manifestations of individuality, but his tastes were for art of a more customary kind, with clear links to classical tradition. Due to this, Fauvism was not yet seen as a whole.

The outlines of the new trend in general, and Fauvism in particular, emerge far more tangibly in the critical comments of those hostile to the Salon des Indépendants. First and foremost they were anarchists striving after the free expression of their individuality, taking a stand against tradition and generally accepted standards of beauty. Colour prevails over the rules of craftsmanship in their paintings, more than that, colour intoxicates them and the paints boil on their canvases. Even the immediate

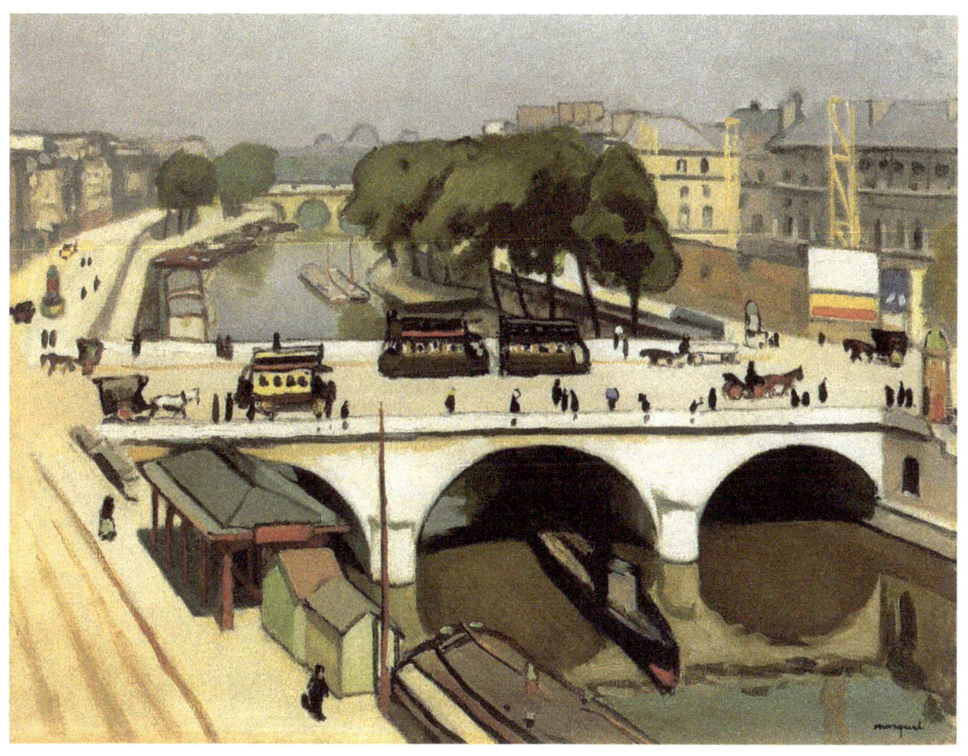

▲ **Albert Marquet**,
The Pont Saint-Michel in Paris, The Quai des Augustins, 1908.
Oil on canvas, 65 x 81 cm. Pushkin State Museum of Fine Arts, Moscow.

sources of their art become clear against the background of this Salon's retrospectives.

Why was Fauvism not distinguished as a phenomenon and given its name here, at the Salon des Indépendants? Suffice it to say that in 1905, 4,269 works were on display, representing 669 artists, twice as many exhibits and exhibitors as the year before. How would the standard-sized canvases of young artists be noticed as the chief quality of which – colour – required light above all things for its effect! As a result, the display by an already completely formed group of a large number of works of what was fully fledged Fauvist art at the 1905 'Salon des Indépendants 'turned out to be no more than a dress rehearsal for the spectacle which took place a few months later at the 'Salon d'Automne '. Little, it would seem, could have changed in that brief interval, nevertheless in the autumn the art of the "wild men" first made a real impact.

Above all, the 'Salon d'Automne ' was truly their exhibition. As a result of the change of membership which took place in 1905, the committee now included, among many others, Matisse, Rouault, Roger-Marx, Vauxcelles and, as proved highly important, a loyal friend and pupil of Gustave Moreau – Georges Desvallières, who became vice-president

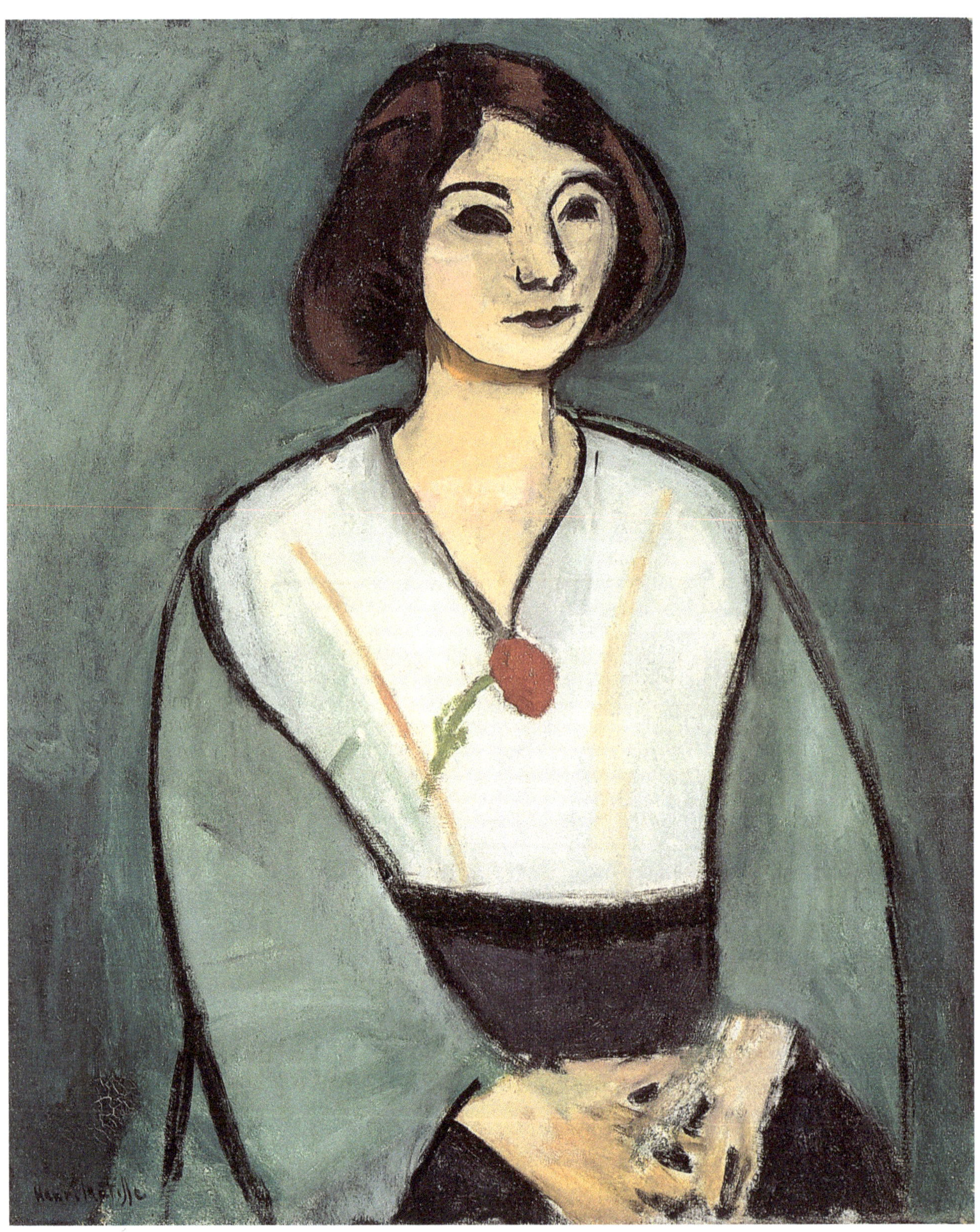

of the Salon. Evidence of the growing authority of the 'Salon d'Automne 'can be found in the scale of the exhibition in 1905: it was enormous – 1,625 works (although still three times less than the Salon des Indépendants). Matisse's group was represented by a smaller number of artists than at the Salon des Indépendants. United by common tastes and strivings, they, without being aware of it themselves, influenced each other, especially if we bear in mind that some of them had worked together previously.

Even more significant was the place they occupied at the exhibition of the 'Salon d'Automne '. In memory of Moreau, Desvallières decided to bring his pupils together – the post of vice-president gave him great opportunities. And that is how the hall appeared, in which side by side were displayed canvases by Matisse, Marquet, Valtat, Manguin, Camoin, and probably also Matisse's friend, Jean Puy. Two writers with attitudes toward the Fauves, which were poles apart, recognized them as a distinct group. Camille Mauclair acknowledged nothing which came after Impressionism, contemptuously called them all artists of the class of Ambroise Vollard, thinking of the "vulgar" tastes of the dealer who had presented Gauguin's work to the Parisian public.

Without doubt, the contrast with the surroundings was intensified to the highest degree by the fact that they took the stage in closed ranks. Matisse, Derain, and Vlaminck were supported by Valtat charmed by the scorching Mediterranean sun, conveying the dazzling brilliance of the Bay of Anthéor, sharp shadows on yellow sand alongside an improbably blue sea, Manguin with landscapes of his beloved south, and even the restrained Marquet. Their painting brought out the very thing inherent in the medium: the capacity of oil paints to set in pastose clots or to spread in a thin layer making it possible for one colour to penetrate into another without losing its purity and resonance in the process. They were united by a genuine, feverish delight in the possibilities offered by a bare canvas and tubes of oil paint – one needs no more than to see Kees van Dongen's *Red Dancer* and Maurice Vlaminck's *Barges* on the Seine alongside each other.

Mockery and insults came from the most varied quarters and expressed themselves in different words, but the meaning boiled down to the same: the Fauves' art was daubing, which had nothing in common with painting; it was denied a place among the creations of normal people and was thus worthy only to be the butt of malicious laughter. In contrast to the Impressionists or Manet, the Fauves belonged to the new twentieth-century generation – mockery and insults did not hurt them, quite the opposite, they received them with satisfaction as a sign of the start of the battle they intended to wage. It must be admitted that in the heat of the battle which had commenced, they set fire to more than they intended. Only a very small amount was necessary for the artists of the official Salons to perish in the flames of the new art – their demise had been prepared by preceding generations. But the strength of the reaction to

◄ **Henri Matisse**,
Woman in Green, 1909.
Oil on canvas, 65 x 54 cm.
State Hermitage Museum, Saint Petersburg.

Matisse's group set both the Nabis and the future innovators in the shade.

Besides this, Fauvism was perceived by enemies and friends alike as a new young force, the only movement which had really come to maturity and one which set itself in opposition to absolutely everything that had existed until that time, both in the "right-wing"camp and on the left. And despite the contradiction within the movement itself, which the critics remarked on, it was a single whole. Even, so it would seem, the incompatible coexistence of spontaneity and rationality became its distinguishing feature, one which no one previously had ever displayed to such a degree. Even their demonstrative taking of the public stage without a leader or a programme united only on the basis of "a spirit of intimate kinship," was, in itself, the program to which most of the Fauvist artists were to adhere all their working lives, far beyond the brief time that is customarily called the Fauvist period.

For the next three years the Fauves used both the 'Salon des Indépendants 'and the 'Salon d'Automne ' for joint displays of their work, each time effectively organizing their own exhibition within the general one. In 1906 they presented about 150 works at the Indépendants and slightly fewer at the 'Salon d'Automne '; in 1907 and 1908, practically unchanged in terms of membership, the group exhibited again, maintaining the same ratio. No less than twice each year the galleries run by Berthe Weill and Druet exhibited Fauves either in groups or singly. Other Parisian dealers also turned their attention to them: apart from his annual personal exhibition of René Seyssaud, in 1908 Bernheim Jeune presented about one hundred works by Kees van Dongen.

From 1906, the Fauves began little by little to become known outside of France. In small groups, most frequently made up of pupils of Moreau, they displayed works at La Libre Esthétique exhibition in Brussels and in a private gallery in Vienna, while in 1910 the Manes Gallery arranged a display of Fauvist painting in Prague. At the 1909 'Salon des Indépendants 'in Paris, the Fauves were again present in full number. At the 'Salon d'Automne ', although their ranks had thinned somewhat, they occupied the central position as before and were now perceived as a single whole.

The peaceful position and conception about the freedom of art which now prevailed no longer prompted them into the fray. The Fauves began a gradual withdrawal – not from the course they had selected, nor from the principles of which they were convinced –from the struggle for a slice of the cake, which, until then, had been divided up by the overwhelming mass of official artists of every hue. One after another they acquired their own regular dealers who provided them with the material wherewithal to live and work; one after another they ceased presenting their creations at collective exhibitions. From 1910 onwards, the number participating in the Fauvist displays at both the 'Salon des Indépendants 'and the 'Salon d'Automne ' steadily declined. The peak of group appearances had passed. Even the name they had won themselves in 1905 did not have the former audacious ring to it: "...the painters who for some time were called les fauves" is how they are described in a very serious review written in the summer of 1910 by a critic close to them – Michel Puy, brother of the painter Jean Puy, who

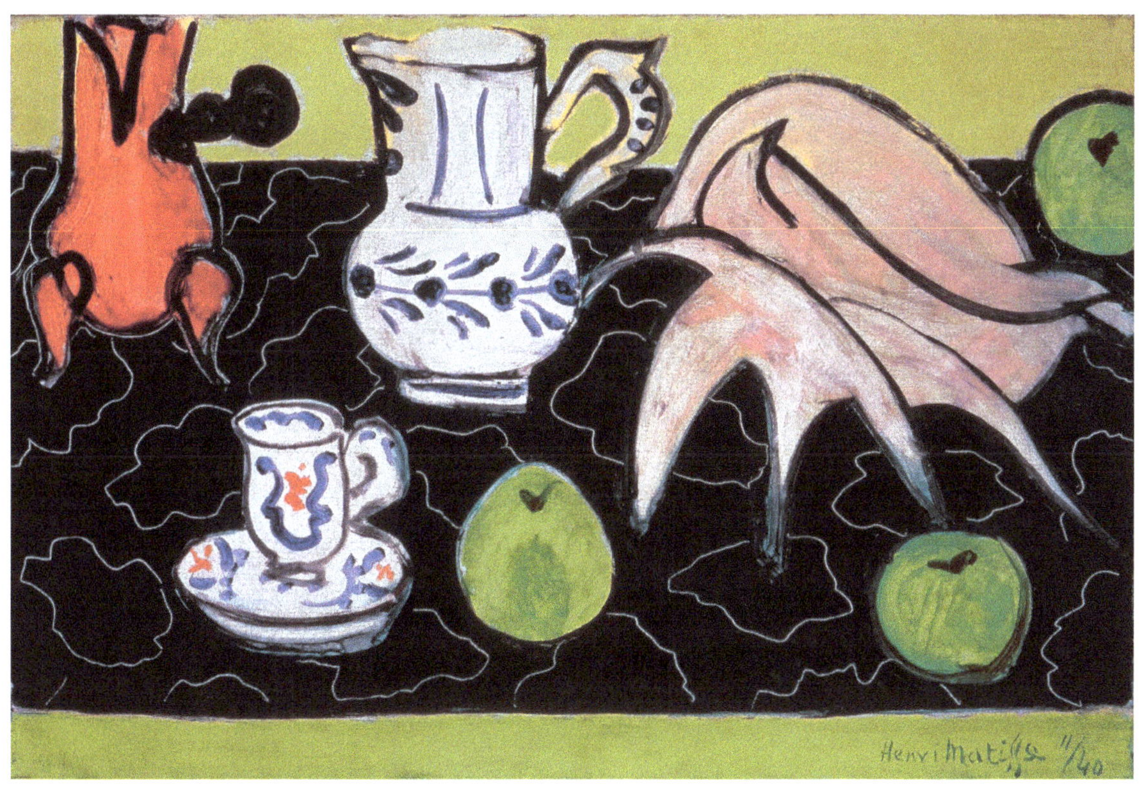

▲ **Henri Matisse**, *Still Life with a Seashell on Black Marble*, 1940.
Oil on canvas, 54 x 81 cm. Pushkin State Museum of Fine Arts, Moscow.

had constantly and closely observed the Fauves development over seven years of joint exhibitions.

Nevertheless, he was not yet ready to draw a final conclusion as to the nature of Fauvism. But Puy considered its most important qualities to be already indisputable. Undoubtedly, the concept of Fauvism includes both, the brief period when the group as well as the qualities of colour common to the painting of the majority. But the mighty impulse, known as Fauvism, which became one of the strongest foundations of twentieth-century painting is in fact far more complex and encompasses a sum total of many qualities. It was precisely the variety of these which attracted artists of very different kinds to Fauvism. It embraced Matisse, who was engrossed in the science of his painting and the spontaneous Vlaminck who provoked the envy of friends from Montmartre for just the opposite reason. And finally, the humblest of the humble, Marquet, who confided to Vlaminck: "I want to become a cab driver! I would earn enough to keep me and while I was waiting for a fare I could draw..."

We can extend the picture – and this unique combination of brilliant personalities already in itself becomes one of the characteristics of Fauvism. With this range of characters, artistic

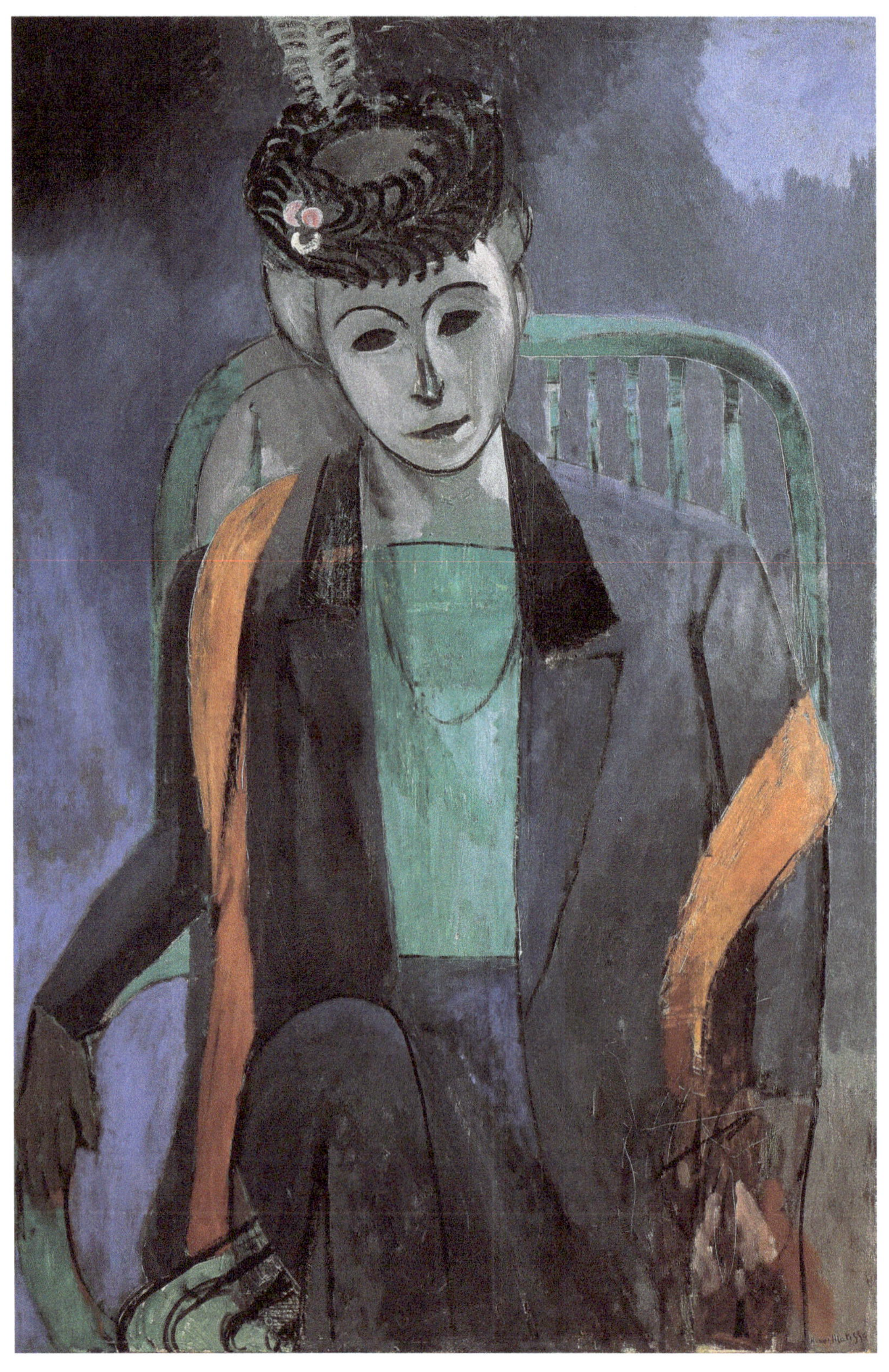

and purely human, for all the highly subjective approach each of them had to evaluate life and art, we nevertheless find in their comments a unity and a certainty with regard to the value of certain characteristics which they jointly acquired.

It not only forces us to listen to the creators of Fauvism, but in all probability in doing so we will also find the answer to the question of what the movement as a whole was about. The Fauves became the only association of artists in the history of art to join together in order to protest their right to work without any sort of common program, declaring their program to be complete freedom for each individual personality, complete creative independence both from any theoretical direction and from their like-minded friends. The turn of a century seems a mere symbolic boundary, yet much did indeed change at the dawn of the twentieth century. The international art world of Paris became so motley and varied, so independent with regard to official artistic life and traditional society that the idea of the artist becoming an outcast completely disappeared, faded into the past together with the nineteenth century. Now the right to individuality in art became something that went without saying and there was no longer any need to unite in defence of it.

Nevertheless they did unite, despite Vlaminck's vehement declaration of his dislike of associations, but not in the least so as to "cross a dangerous spot."

◀ **Henri Matisse**,
Portrait of the Artist's Wife, 1913.
Oil on canvas, 146 x 97.7 cm.
State Hermitage Museum, Saint Petersburg.

They needed to proclaim the creed of individual freedom loudly and that was best done in chorus. Because, if we try to be precise, it must be admitted that they formed neither a school, nor even a group as such. True, they were called Matisse's group, but that designation appeared in the press only in order to have some way of setting them apart and defining them. There was no group; they never assembled especially to decide common questions.

Although they were called Matisse's group, the reason was not the role he played in the organization of the association. He did not dictate a program to anyone and did not oblige anyone to follow in his footsteps. The probable impetus for this was the system of painting which was specifically Matisse's, the achievement of harmony in painting through the juxtaposition of patches of pure colour. And if a leader needed to be found, the most reliable thing was to let one's choice settle on the artist whose works betrayed a theoretical basis. That, however, was no more than the view from outside. When we are thinking of the coming together of the Fauves, would it not make more sense to postulate the leadership of "le plus authentique des Fauves"[the most authentic Beasts]– Maurice de Vlaminck who himself declared: "Ce qu'est le fauvisme? C'est moi!"[What is Fauvism? It's me!] But Vlaminck was never the head of the group either, they really did not have a leader, and not in the least because there was no-one among them capable of taking the lead – it simply contradicted the very essence of Fauvism.

There could be no other program; they met any suggestion that something else existed with protest.

"We had no doctrine, any of us," Van Dongen stated. In denying the existence of a doctrine. Van Dongen here in fact confirmed a principle important for Fauvism. On the one hand, their painting proceeded directly from that of the Impressionists for whom they felt sincere respect. On the other hand, the Fauves occupied an anti-Impressionist position, just as they were anti-Nabis, as had already been noted by the critics at the time. It was no mere chance that contemporary researchers compare Fauvism with Delacroix's painting, all the more so since the Fauves turned to him in a completely conscious manner. It is true the Impressionists' revelation of the possibilities of pure colour, the unconstrained and expressive aspect of texture, were a stage which led to the emergence of the Fauves' chromatic approach.

Van Gogh, Gauguin, and Cézanne brought painting to a position where accumulated ideas about the possibilities of creating with paints had to be resolved in a flood of new works. And the means of the Fauves protests against being considered Impressionists, te hub in which all their charges against their predecessors were concentrated, became colour, which attained such an intensity and expressive force that all other means faded into the background alongside it. Colour became the banner of the Fauves, the symbol of the liberation of their painting from all fetters. It was a part of that very programme, the existence of which they denied.

The Fauves' colour carried optimism within it in contrast to that of their German Expressionist contemporaries. To them, one thing that remained unshakeable in painting was that it was born out of life and reflected life which was its true source. "The goal we set ourselves is happiness, a happiness which consequently we should create," Derain said. In order to create it, one must have a love of life itself, be endowed with that "Flemish sense of joy" which Apollinaire found in Vlaminck's painting. "I love life more than anything," Jean Puy bashfully confessed.

At the start of the century the Fauves were the first to proclaim preference for the intuitive course in painting; the power of the painterly element over the artistic, as one of the inseparable qualities of the freedom after which they were striving. Even the most rational of them – Matisse, who was most inclined to make experiments in painting on a par with scientific research – asserted: "It is through colour that I feel." Despite its many-layered complexity, Fauvism had an entirely definite orientation. Cubism, which appeared alongside after an interval of two years, not only overshadowed Fauvism, but also placed both phenomena in a definite position in the general historical succession. Cubism appeared as a variety of Classicism, superseding the Romanticism of the Fauves. Both these currents continued to flow in parallel, gathering strength in turns, overtaking one another, changing in form but retaining their essence.

No small part of the significance of Fauvism lies in the fact that, created by young artists

▶ **Henri Matisse,**
Moroccan in Green, 1913.
Oil on canvas, 146.5 x 97.7 cm.
State Hermitage Museum, Saint Petersburg.

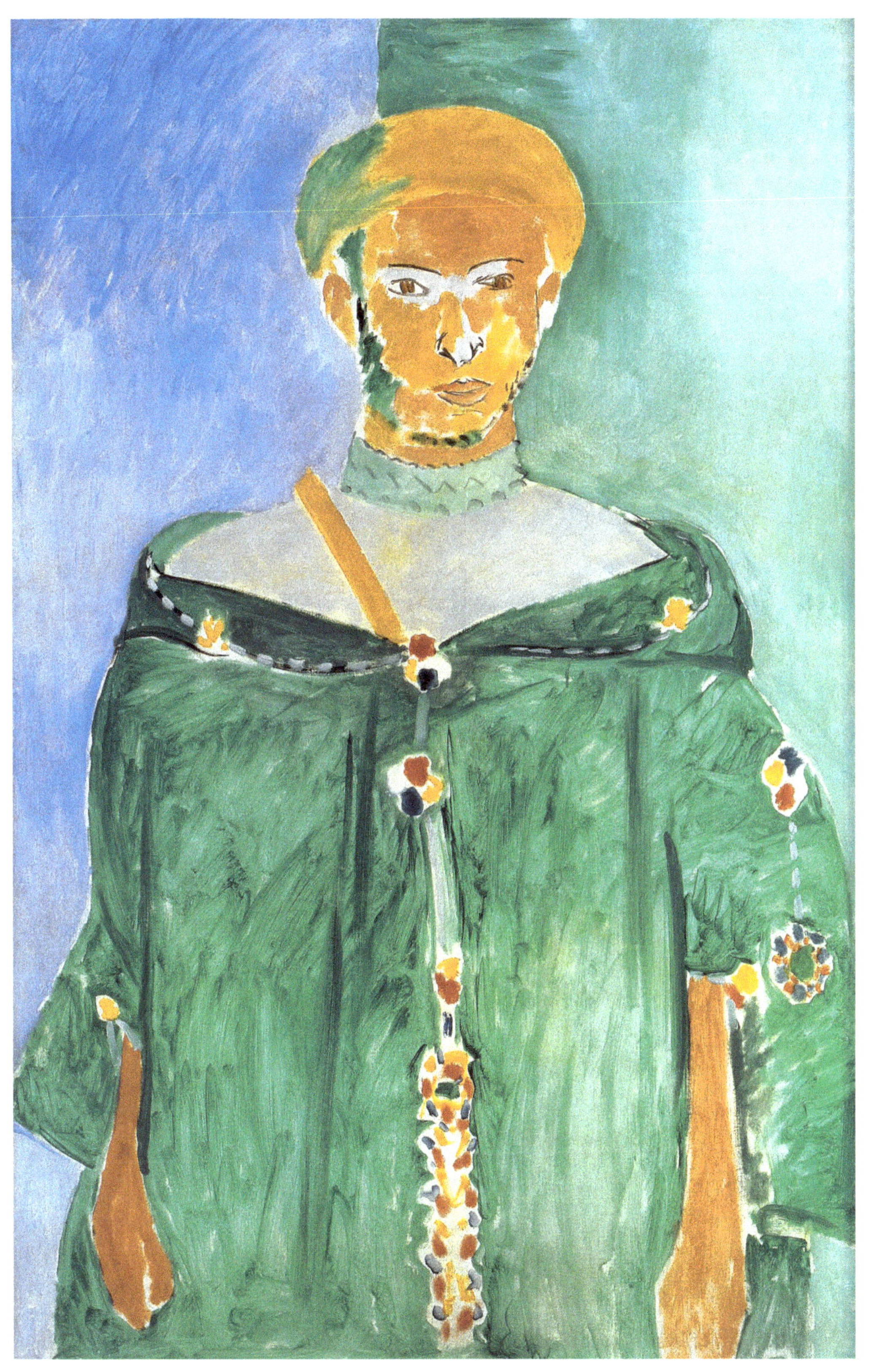

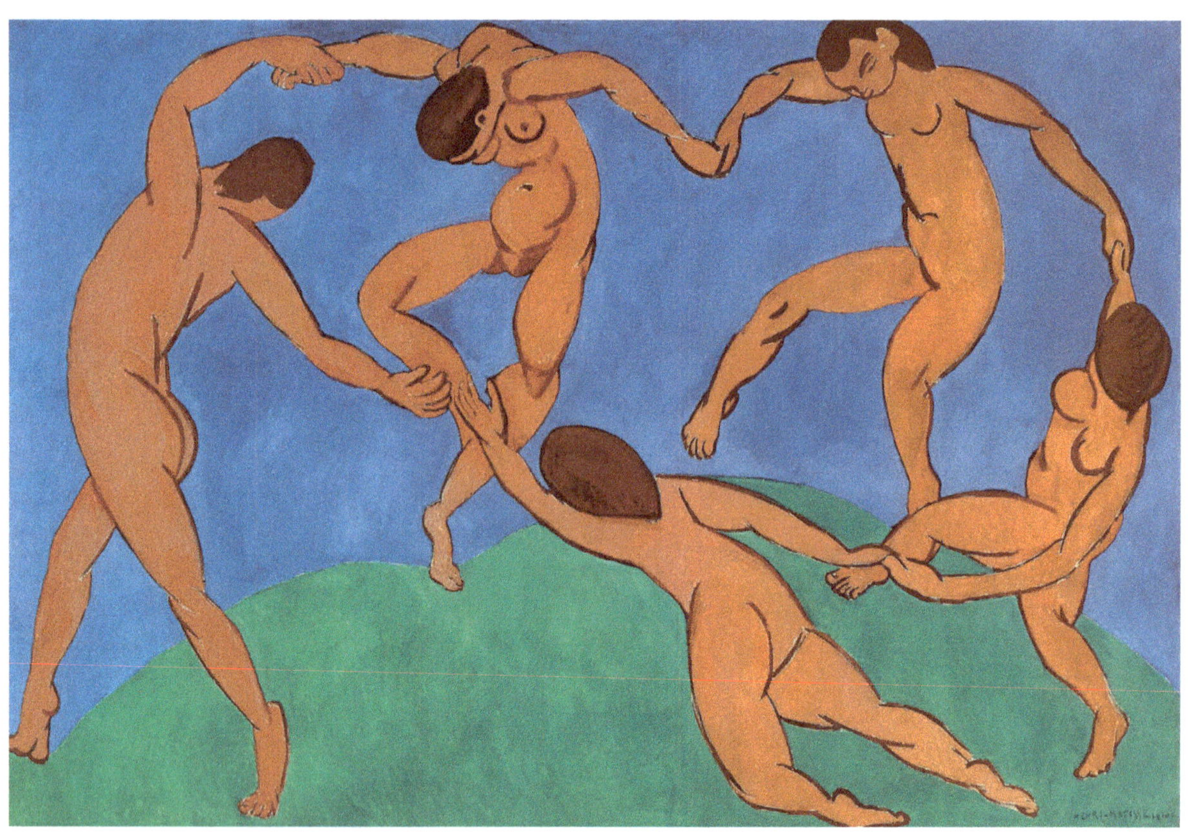

▲ **Henri Matisse**, *The Dance*, 1909-1910.
Oil on canvas, 260 x 391 cm. State Hermitage Museum, Saint Petersburg.

at the turn of the century, it became, in turn, a medium that nourished and educated them. Fauvism signified a path of natural development without any kind of force or compulsion. It taught the ability to listen to oneself, to take a pride in what was one's own, the individual, and to hold firmly to it. Leaving aside the eloquent examples of Matisse and Van Dongen, we must pay tribute to the courage of Dufy, Marquet, Puy, Manguin or Chabaud – their work became the embodiment of precisely that which Vlaminck said in verse: "The nightingale doesn't sing into the phonograph."

The range of the Fauves' creativity is fairly broad, encompassing everything, which came into an artist's field of vision at the beginning of the twentieth century. Although they began as "anti-Nabis," it was the Nabis who gave the Fauves an interest in applied and graphic art. These spheres had a need for real artists and Matisse's generation possessed a large stock of energy. The primacy of colour in Fauvist painting prompted the idea of decorative art from the outset. Almost all the Fauves went through a phase of being interested in applied art, but neither Fauvism in general nor the artists themselves lost their individuality.

None of the Fauves overlooked either the graphic arts, beginning with the newspaper and magazine caricatures with which many of them earned money in their youth, through the drawings, watercolours, and gouaches, which naturally accompanied their work throughout their lives, to prints and book illustrations. If one regards Fauvism only as a period of shared enthusiasm for the element of colour, graphic art would seem to have only a fairly tenuous connection with it. As a major phenomenon in the fine arts in general, as a continuation of the tendencies and lines of Romanticism in the twentieth century, Fauvism gave a powerful impulse to all forms of art. Even Derain's quick pen-and-ink drawings carry in them a sense of vital force and thoroughness characteristic of the "school of Château." Every one of Marquet's landscape sketches possesses the constancy, modesty, and restraint which were the hallmark of his painting. Raoul Duty's prints are sincere and naive. Vlaminck's wood engravings are spontaneous, unrestrained, and energetic. As far as Matisse's astonishing line is concerned, immediate and free, yet at the same time precise and thoroughly considered, it was perhaps the very thing which drew the critics' attention to the particular role drawing played for the Fauves. The book called *Jazz* (Paris, 1937), which Matisse created at the end of his life, demonstrates in its integrity of conception and unity in the assembling of pictorial means all the qualities of Fauvism with no less force than the painting of his youth.

Fauvism started life together with the twentieth century – a sober, technical century full of complex machinery and immense speeds, the most savage of wars, violence against nature and man. In the twentieth century, in art, too, more or less significant new systems began to appear one after another, beginning with Cubism, Futurism, and Surrealism, systems less enduring but not in the slightest less strict and tyrannical than Classicism. The very fact of their presence, the formation of definite groupings around them naturally evoked reaction. In each generation there are young artists who tend towards intuitive, spontaneous, and sincere self-expression. It is a characteristic of many of them that they strive to link themselves with the Fauvist tradition – there are even echoes in the names they give themselves, be it the "Neue Wilden" in Germany or some groups that appeared in Paris, St Petersburg, or Moscow. For us, the Impressionists, Van Gogh, and Cézanne are almost as distant as Rembrandt and Rubens. They have entirely withdrawn to the museums, but Matisse, Vlaminck, Dufy, Van Dongen, Rouault, and Manguin belong to the twentieth century.

"Fauvism is when there is a red," said Henri Matisse concisely putting into words the most straightforward notion held of Fauvism. Matisse has in fact become Fauvism's leader over the years as a result of his contemporaries and researchers persistently perpetuating such an idea. Consequently, Matisse's work has been scoured through in a search for the ultimate Fauvist painting. Matisse never pretended or aspired to such a role, and on the question of what Fauvism represents in theory and in practice, he never came to a final conclusion. With the other Fauvists it can be argued that their art was dominated by either reason or emotion. Matisse's intellect, however, continuously searched for a direction where both reason and emotion became reconciled so balance and order might be found.

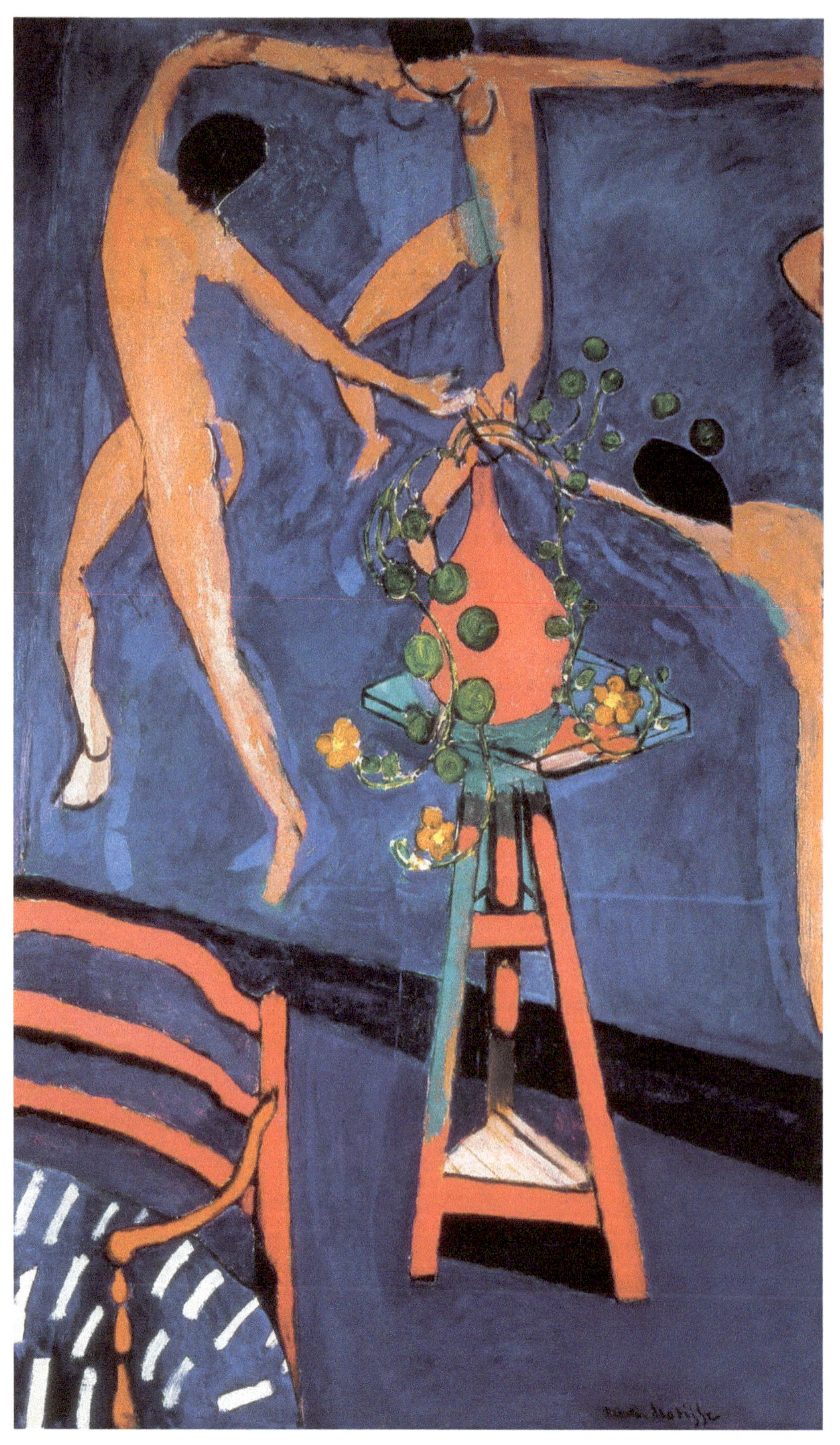

THE ARTISTS

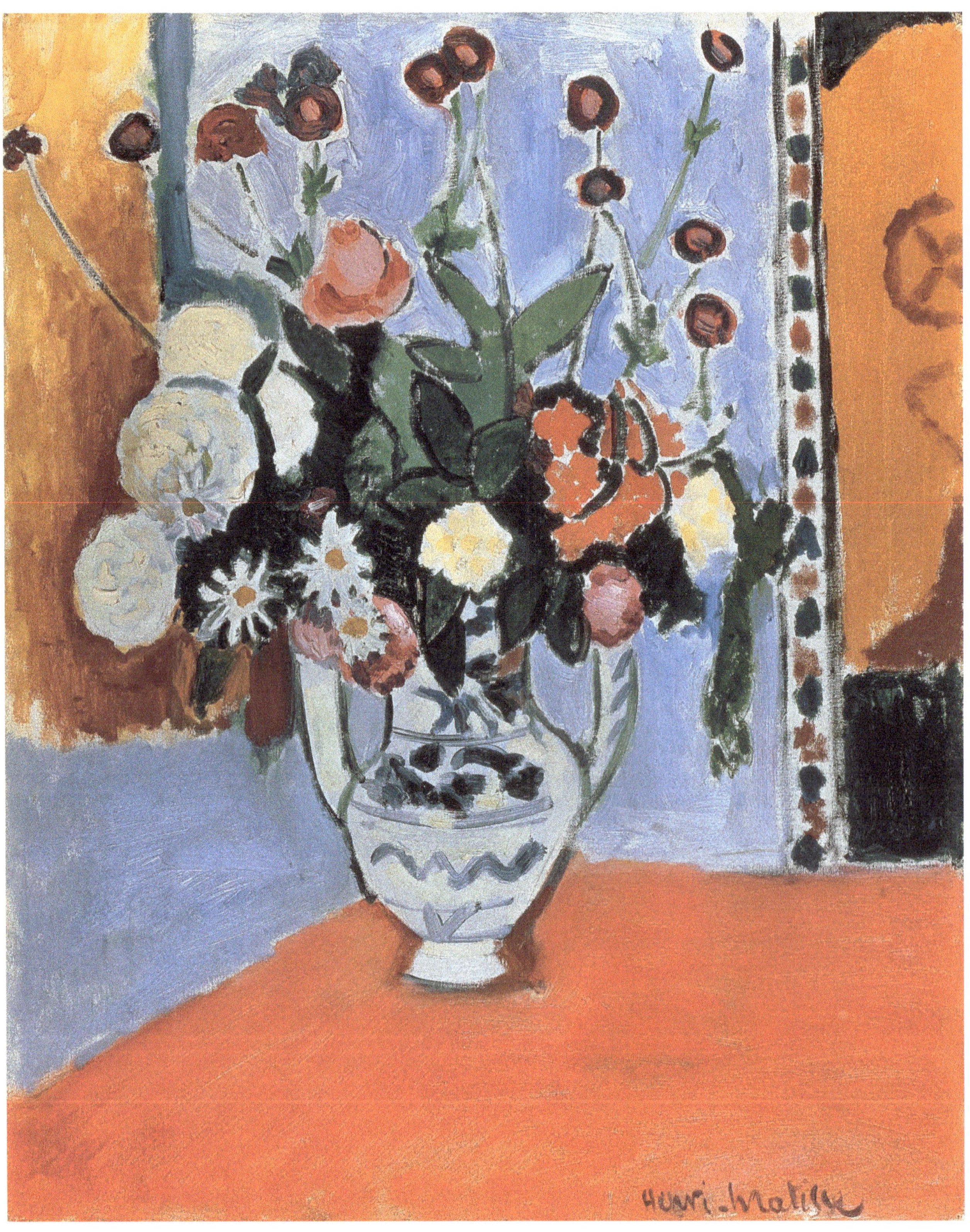
Henri-Matisse

HENRI MATISSE

(1869 CATEAU-CAMBRÉSIS – 1954 NICE)

Henri Matisse was born on 31 December 1869 into a stallholder's family in Cateau-Cambrésis in northern France. He began his education at the secondary school in Saint-Quentin and continued at Paris University where he read law. Upon graduating, he returned to Saint-Quentin where he worked in a lawyer's office. During this period Matisse began to attend his first drawing classes and at the age of twenty, when an illness confined him to bed for nearly a year, he painted his first work.

Matisse started to take lessons at the 'Académie Julian' in 1891, working as a law tutor to help pay his way. In 1892 he abandoned Bouguereau's totally uninspiring lessons and transferred to Gustave Moreau's classes at the 'Ecole des Beaux-Arts'. During the evenings Matisse also attended classes in applied art and there he made friends with Albert Marquet, who soon also became a pupil of Moreau. It was at these classes that a group of artists came together and formed friendships that would endure all the trials and tribulations of their respective lives. This group consisted of the "Three M's" – Matisse, Marquet and Manguin – as well as Georges Rouault, Charles Camoin and Louis Valtat. Working in Léon Bonnat's studio, which was just across the corridor, was another future member, Othon Friesz. And he would later be joined by Raoul Dufy. In 1901 Matisse and his friends started to exhibit their work at the Salon des Indépendants and in Berthe Weill's gallery. In 1903 they were involved in the founding of the Salon d'Automne, where two years later Vauxcelles would see their work and dub them "les fauves".

The Salon d'Automne scandal over *Woman with a Hat* in 1905 brought Matisse fame and glory at a time when the preceding generation of artists were only just beginning to receive theirs. Matisse, as a natural inheritor of the French tradition, showed himself more than respectful of his elders.

▲ **Henri Matisse,**
Nasturtiums with 'Dance' (II), 1912.
Oil on canvas, 109.5 x 112 cm.
Pushkin State Museum of Fine Arts, Moscow. (p. 24)

◄ **Henri Matisse,**
Bouquet (Vase with Two Handles), 1907.
Oil on canvas, 74 x 61 cm.
State Hermitage Museum, Saint Petersburg.

The chain of thought which brought Matisse to *The Dance* and *Music* can be traced within the two major Russian collections. In the 1908 painting, A *Game of Boules*, now in Hermitage, Matisse tried to resolve two issues: first, decorative abstraction with a strong concentration of colour – dark blue, green and ochre yellow; second, the creation on the surface of the canvas of a balanced form based upon the classical triangle. The direction taken in colour was continued in *Nymph and Satyr*. However, this painting also saw the introduction into the classical pyramid of crisp and vigorous arched lines capable of giving a painting balance in combination with the motion of the figures which it contains.

"Fauvism is when there is a red," said Henri Matisse concisely putting into words the most straightforward notion held of Fauvism. Matisse has in fact become Fauvism's leader over the years as a result of his contemporaries and researchers persistently perpetuating such an idea. Consequently Matisse's oeuvre has been scoured through in a search for the ultimate Fauvist painting. Matisse never pretended or aspired to such a role, and on the question of what Fauvism represents in theory and in practice, he never came to a final conclusion.

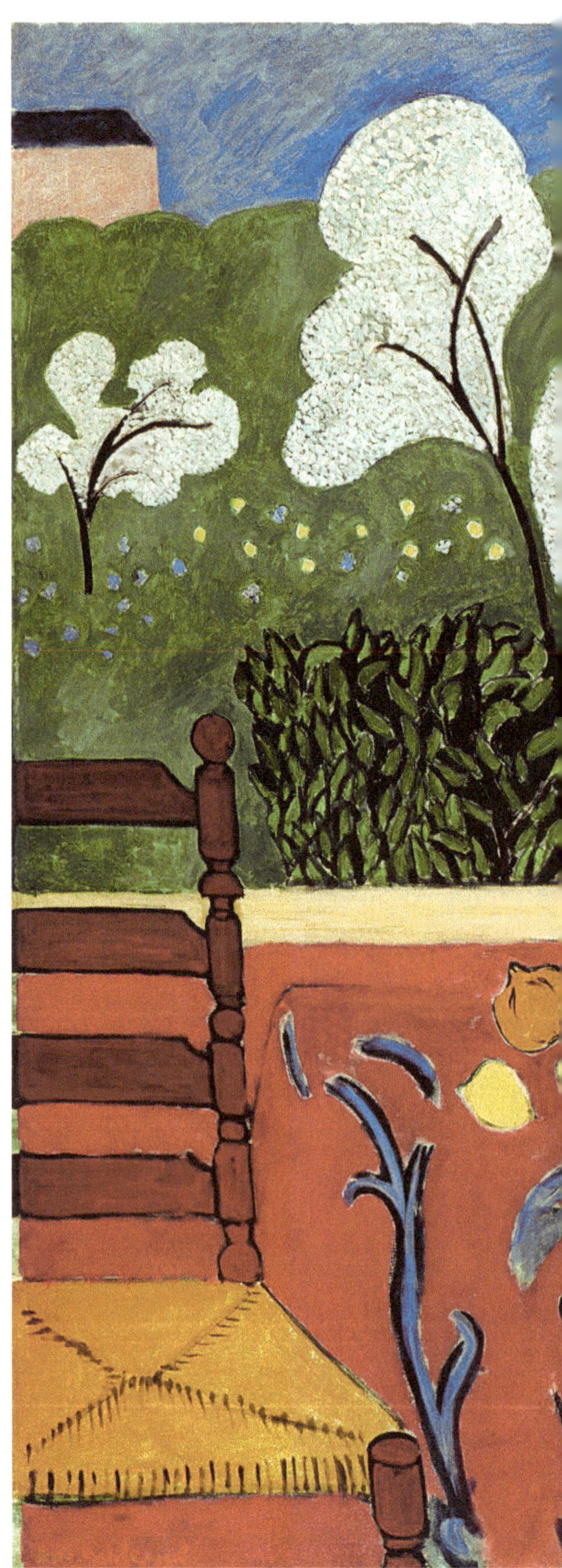

▶ **Henri Matisse,**
The Red Room (Harmony in Red), 1908.
Oil on canvas, 180.5 x 221 cm.
State Hermitage Museum, Saint Petersburg.

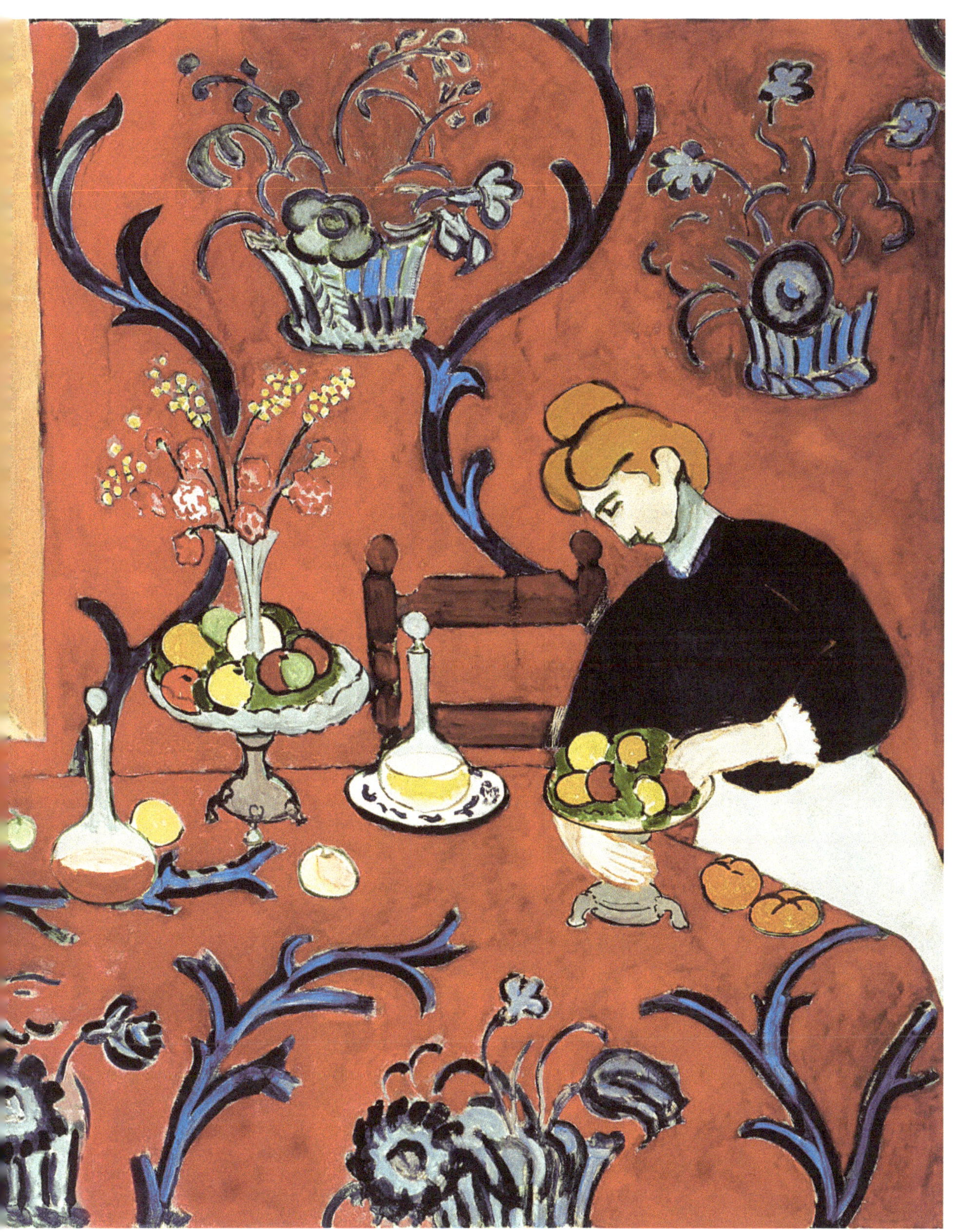

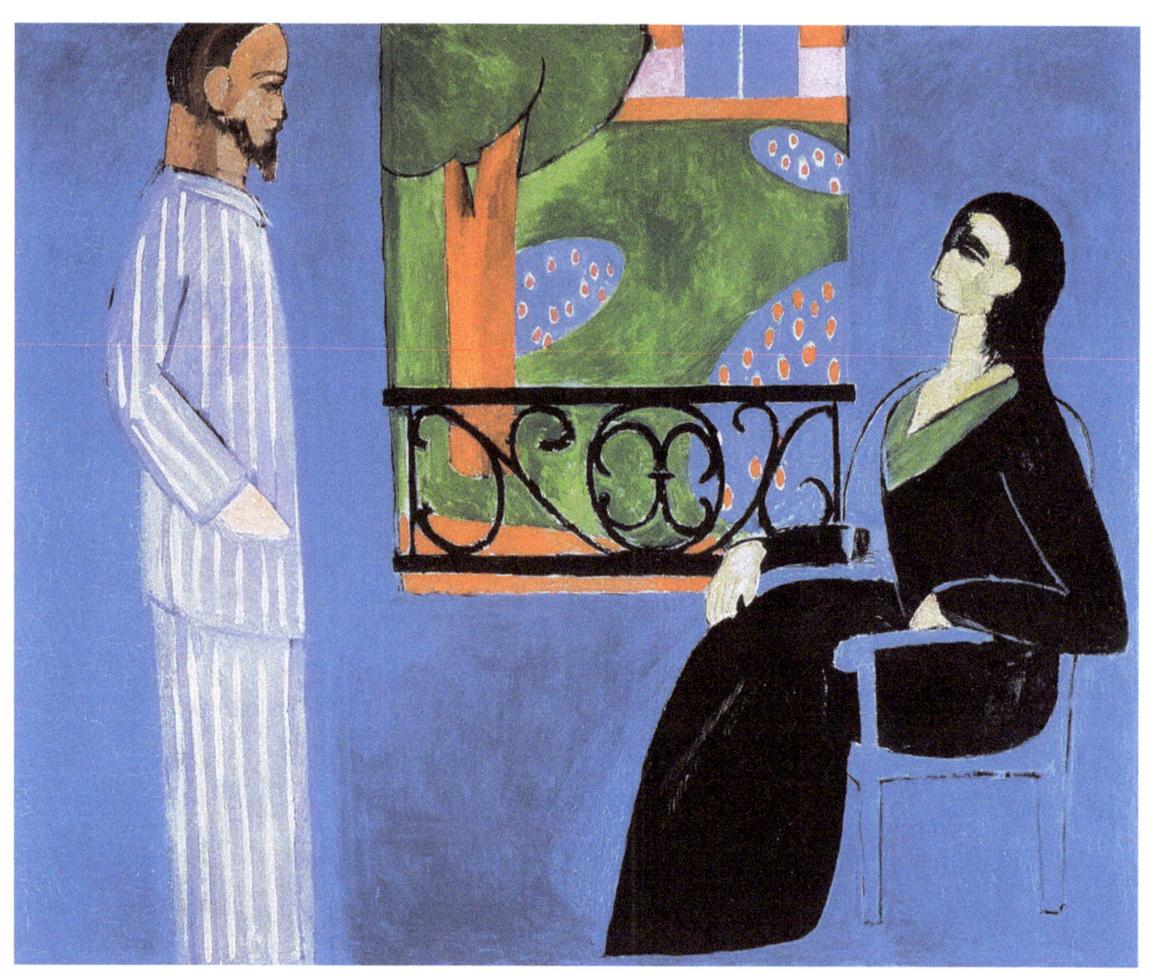

▲ **Henri Matisse,**
Conversation, 1908-1912.
Oil on canvas, 177 x 217 cm.
State Hermitage Museum, Saint Petersburg.

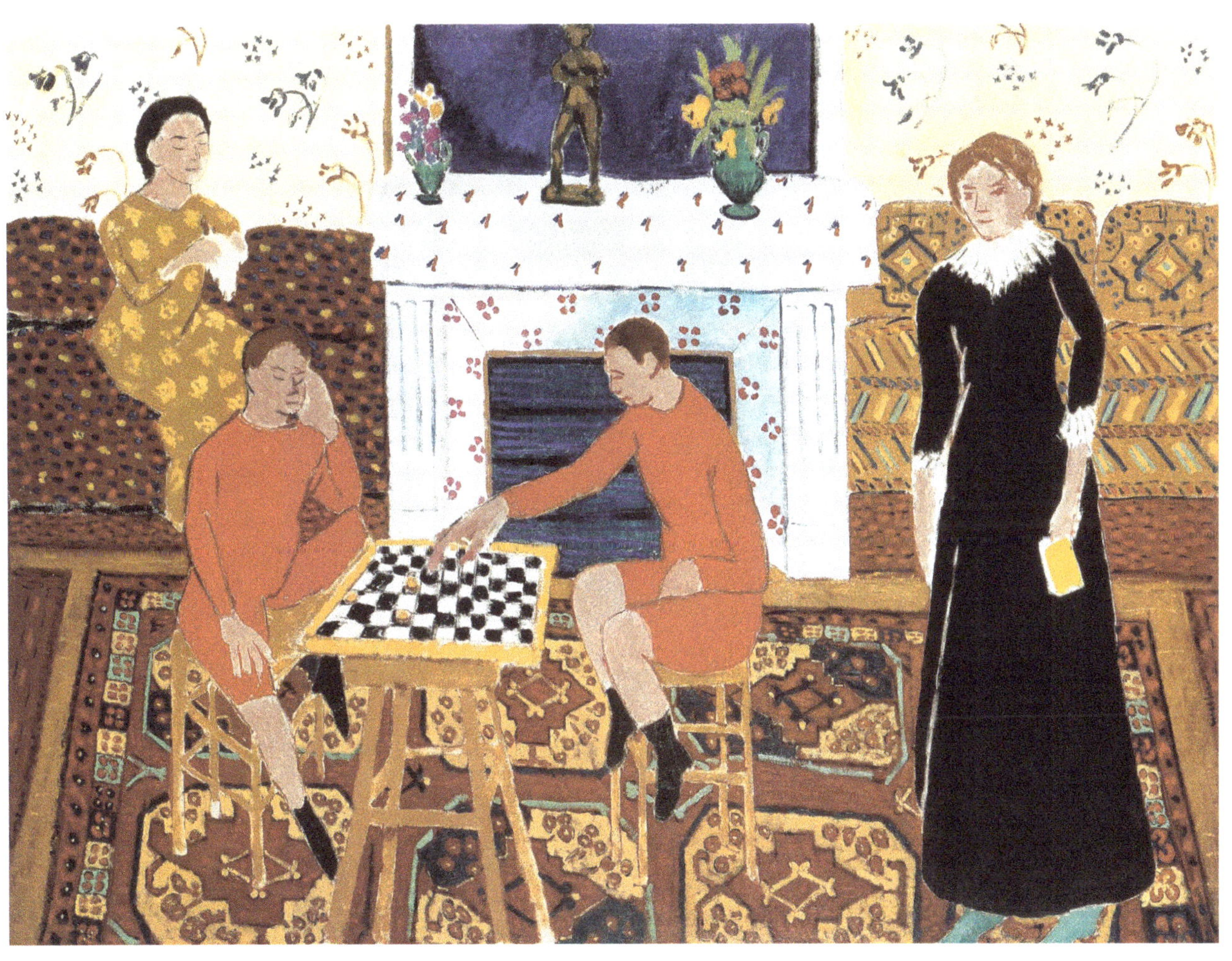

▲ **Henri Matisse,**
Painter's Family, 1911.
Oil on canvas, 143 x 194 cm.
State Hermitage Museum, Saint Petersburg.

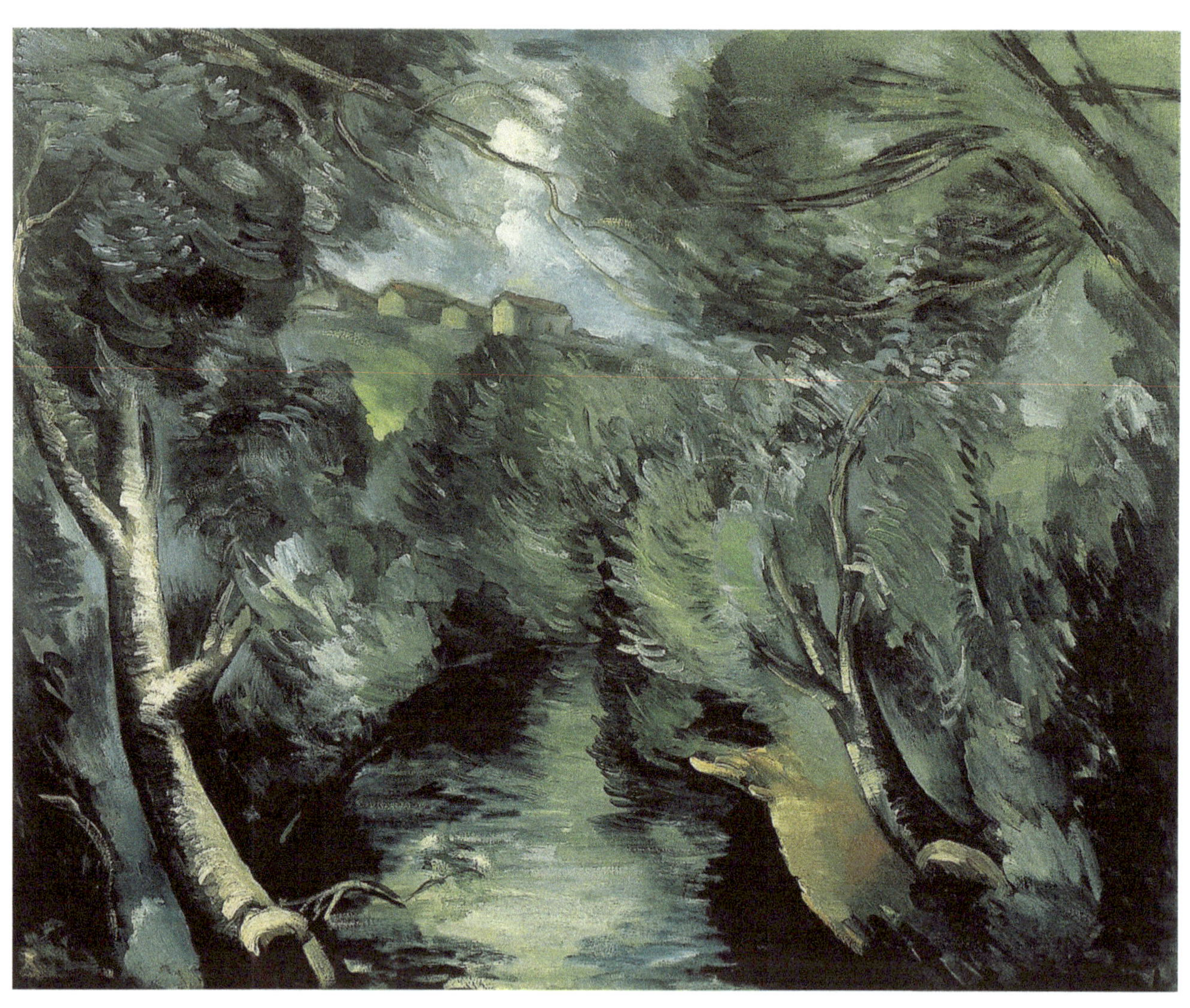

▲ **Maurice de Vlaminck**,
Landscape with River, 1912.
Oil on canvas, 83 x 102 cm.
Pushkin State Museum of Fine Arts, Moscow.

MAURICE DE VLAMINCK

(1876 PARIS – 1958 RUEIL-LA-GADELIERE)

For Vlaminck, born into a family of music teachers in Paris on 4 August 1876, it seemed natural to earn a living through music. The friends of his youth remembered him playing the violin like a gypsy in the taverns of the Parisian suburbs. Moreover, he constantly had to give music lessons because, at the age of twenty-one, he was already married with two small children. Entirely self-taught, Vlaminck doubted that he could make a living from painting until he met André Derain by coincidence, who became a real friend.

At the 1905 'Salon d'Automne ', the Fauves, especially Vlaminck and Matisse, were derided by the critics for their expressive style of drawing and their riotous use of colour and textured painting. Vlaminck, as an anarchist nihilist, was naturally delighted rather than dismayed at their response. Up until this time he would very occasionally receive ridiculously small sums for his pictures, but in 1905 Ambroise Vollard bought the entire contents of his studio for 6,000 francs and signed him up for a five-year contract. The money enabled Vlaminck to buy a small house in Bougival and finally to dedicate himself solely to painting.

In 1907 Vollard organized Vlaminck's first one-man exhibition, but in 1912 he changed dealers signing a contract with Kahnweiler. In 1913, the last year of peace in Europe before the First World War, he and Derain went on a painting tour to the south of France. The war broke the momentum of his nascent artistic career.

Two early works, *View of the Seine* and *Barges on the Seine*, came into Ivan Morozov's collection from Vollard and it is quite likely that they were in Vlaminck's studio when Vollard bought the entire contents. *View of the Seine* (1906, Hermitage), depicting the river bank near the Chatou Bridge (a spot where Vlaminck often worked before moving to Bougival). Vlaminck's painting, constructed on the parallel, almost horizontal lines of the boats and bank, looks quieter and there are no figures in the foreground adding life.

The artist produced many landscapes in the 1920s and Landscape with *A House on a Hill* is probably not one of the more outstanding examples. Nevertheless, it reveals the maturity of the painter. From a fairly restrained palette of greens, browns, yellows and greys Vlaminck manages to extract a seemingly infinite range of rich colours and tones. A stripe of yellow ochre brings light into the picture. Vlaminck no longer squeezed primary colours directly from the tube onto the canvas, his

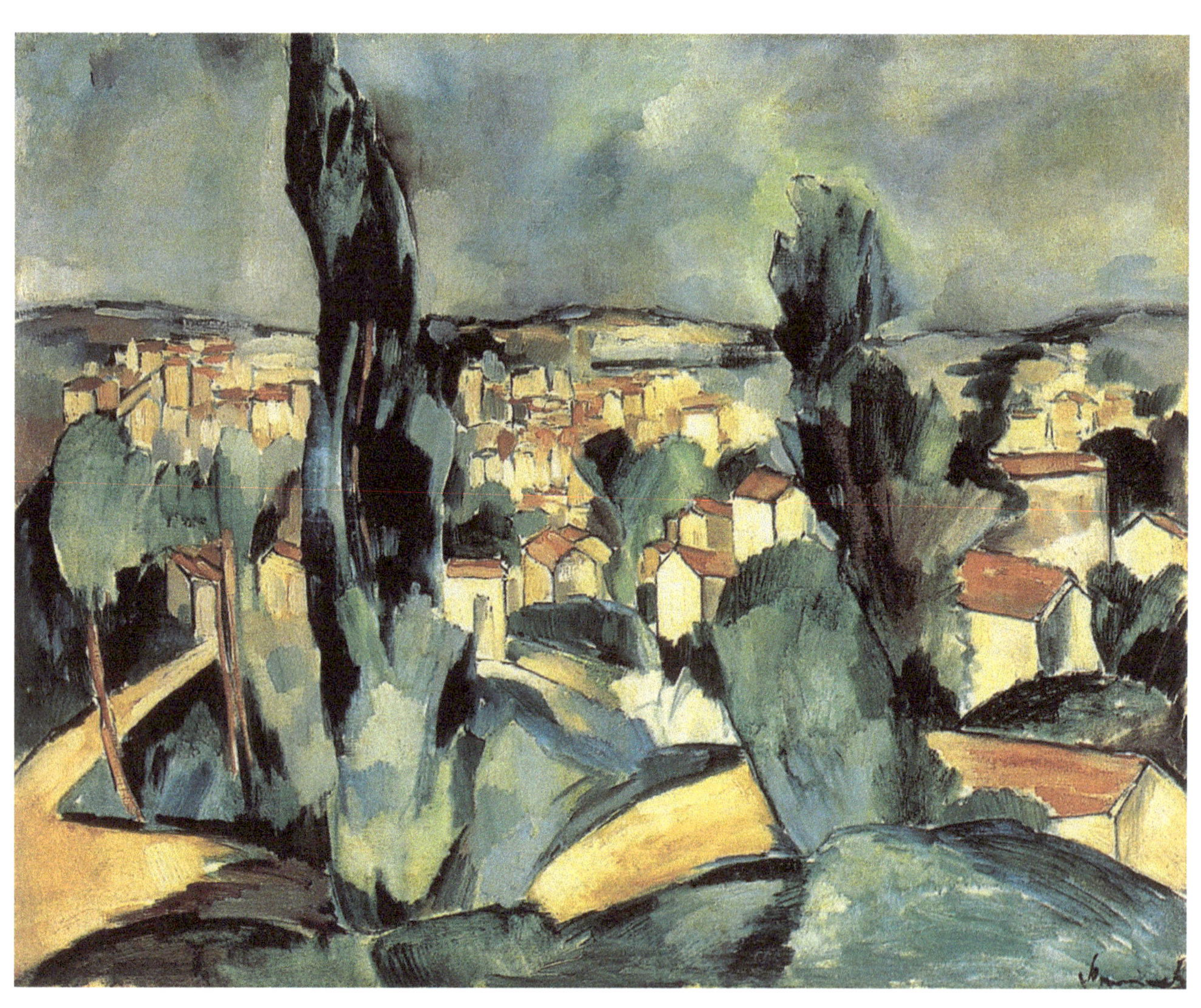

▲ **Maurice de Vlaminck**,
Town, c. 1908-1909.
Oil on canvas, 73.4 x 92.3 cm.
State Hermitage Museum, Saint Petersburg.

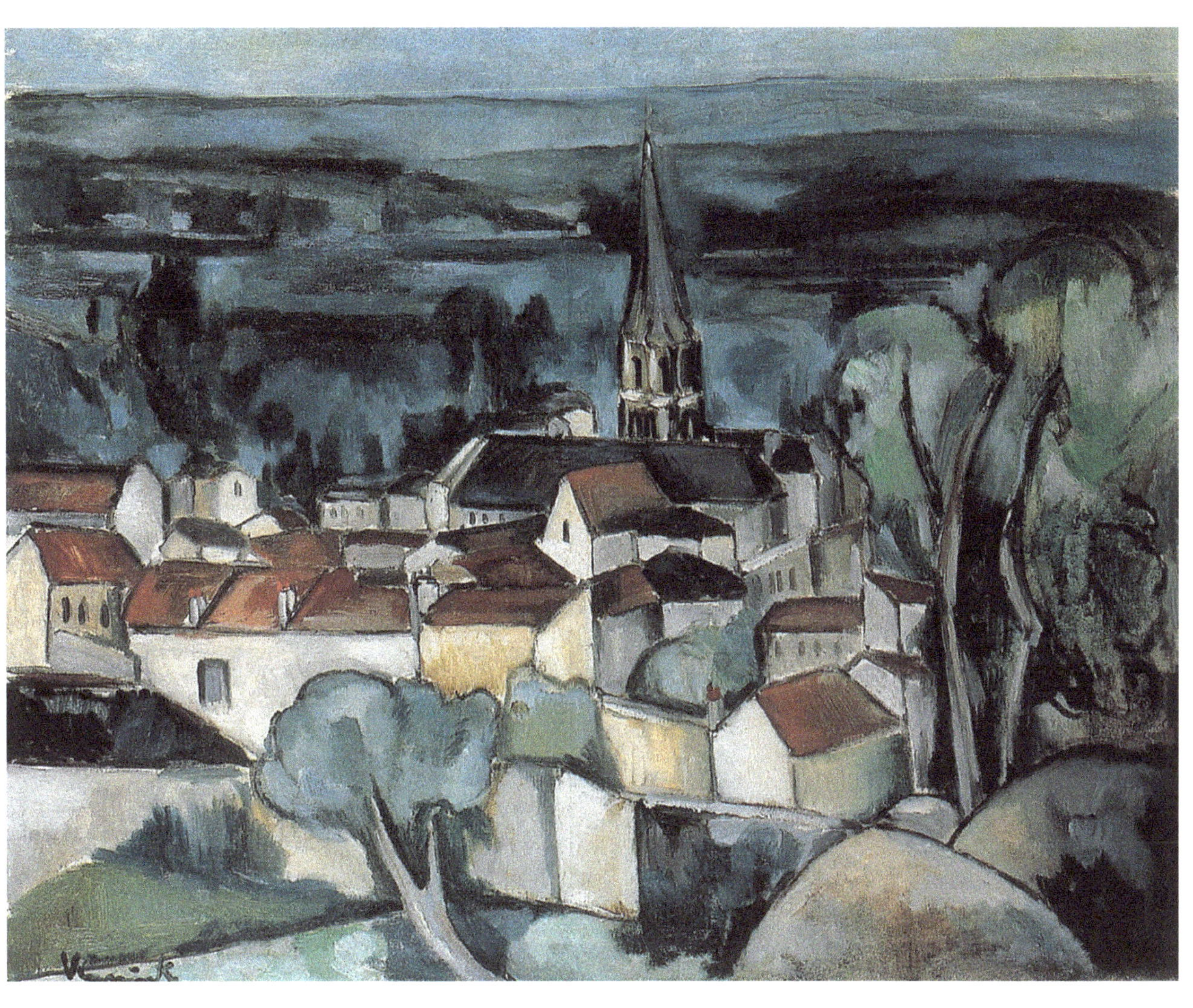

▲ **Maurice de Vlaminck**,
Bougival, c. 1909.
Oil on canvas, 73 x 92 cm.
State Hermitage Museum, Saint Petersburg.

approach was more orderly and methodical, but in spite of this, the colour is still the most dominant element of the work.

It is often stated in biographies of Vlaminck that the 1950s saw him return to his wild, Fauvist style. But *Landscape at Auvers*, *Landscape with a House on a Hill* and many others like them, painted at the same time, are proof that he never entirely abandoned his wild manner. *Landscape at Auvers* is Vlaminck, yet again, expressing his temperament through colour and surface texture. The linear design is slightly blurred and patches of green float slightly on the road. Soft brush movements describe the foliage of the trees, the impasto layers lying so thick that the very surface of the painting seems to vibrate. This work contains everything: the physical and plastic qualities of drawing and form; the transparent air; the infinite varieties of shade and hue evoking living nature and a sense of movement

Vlaminck's life was a reflection of his character, straightforward, sincere, often unrestrained and harsh. He did not change over the years. Only one hour by car from Paris, on 'La Tourillière', he lived out his days with Berthe Combe and their two daughters, sometimes going away but never for long, painting pictures and writing novels. He died from a serious illness in 1958 in the bosom of his family, mourned by friends and neighbours.

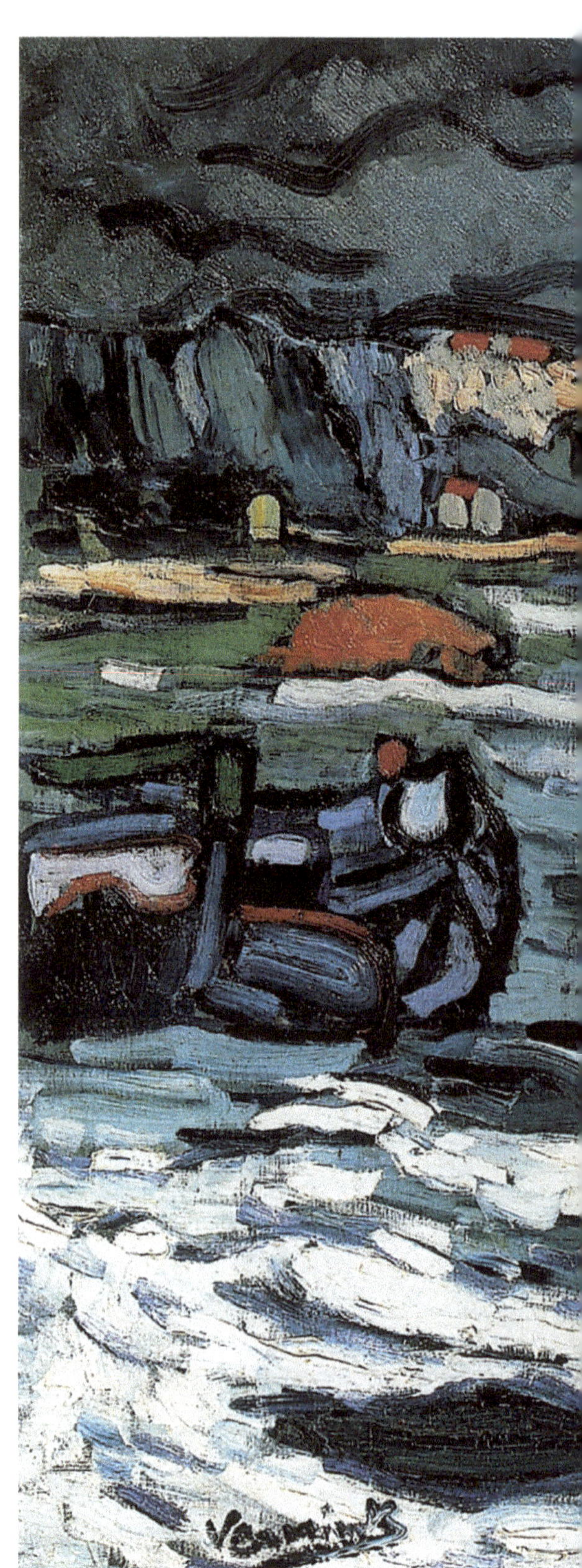

▶ **Maurice de Vlaminck,**
A Barge on the Seine River, 1905-1906.
Oil on canvas, 81 x 100 cm.
Pushkin State Museum of Fine Arts, Moscow.

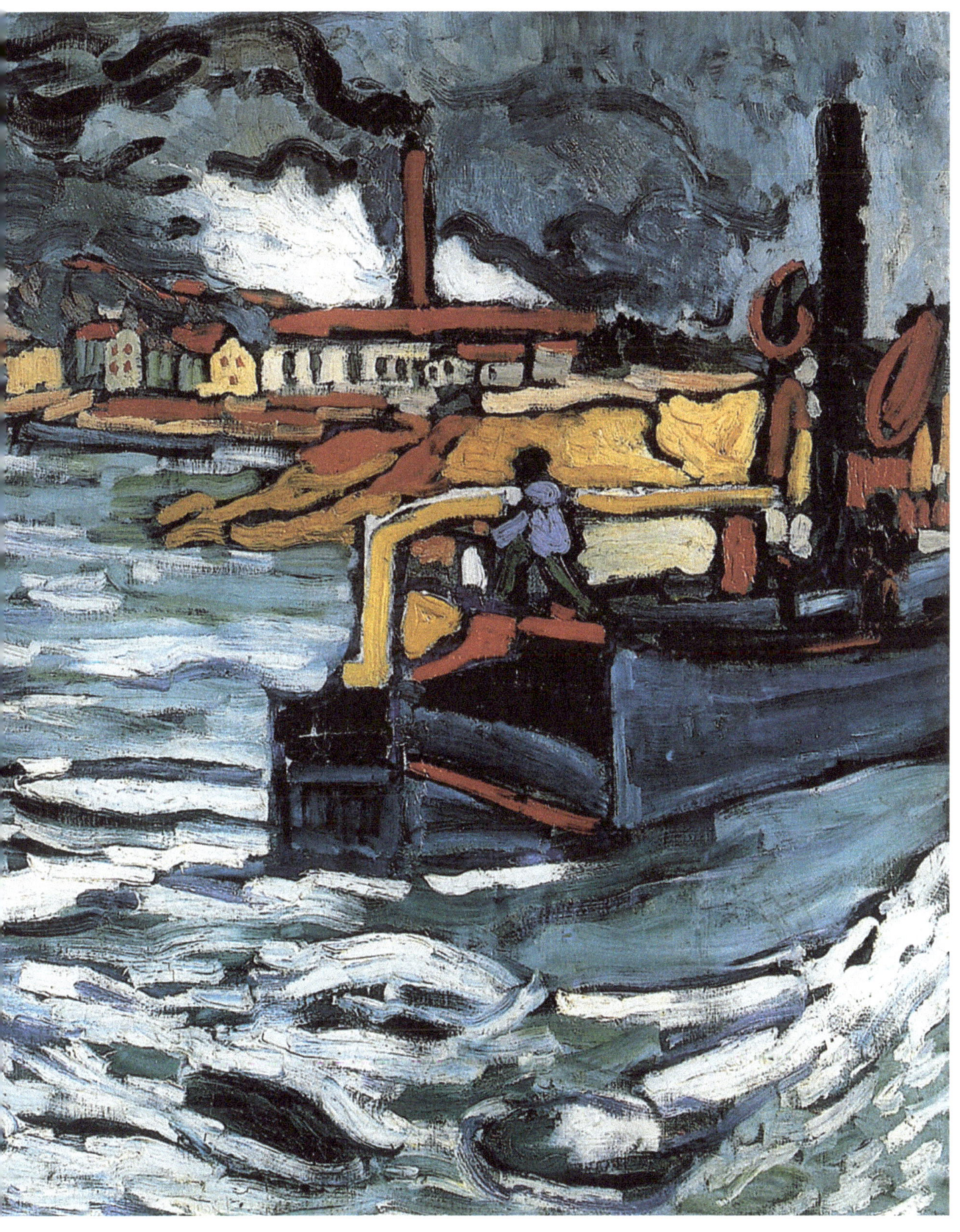

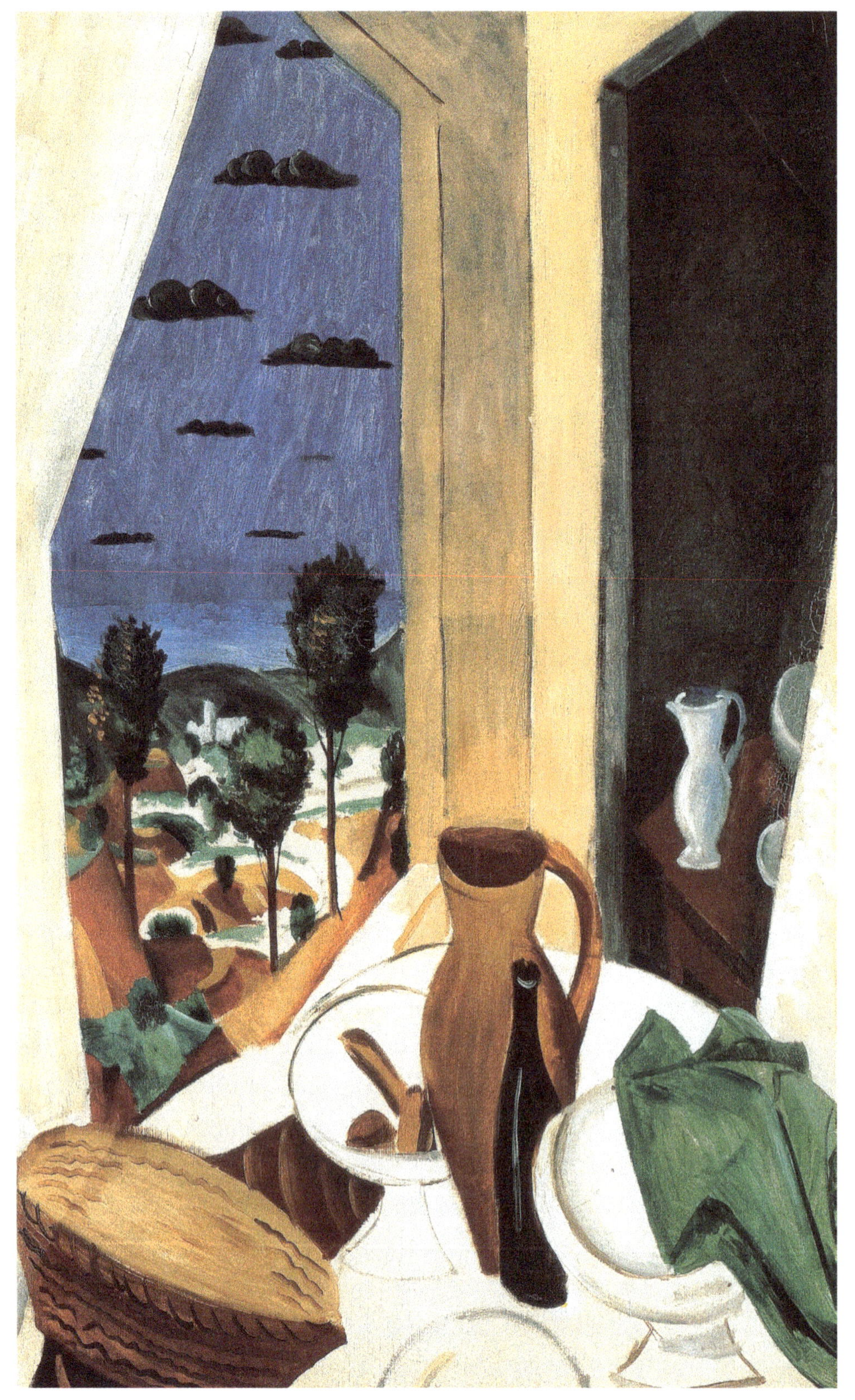

ANDRÉ DERAIN

(1880 CHATOU – 1954 GARCHES)

André Derain was born on 17 June 1880 in the Parisian suburb of Chatou. An important friendship was struck in 1898 when Derain met Vlaminck on a suburban train going from Paris to Chatou. The two immediately recognized the close similarity of their interests: they simply could not live without art. Both of them had grown up in poor, hard-working families. And both of them were large-framed and powerfully built; both were full of energy and a determination to upset conventions wherever possible.

Derain joined the Matisse group for the 'Salon d'Automne ' exhibition and even spent the summer of 1905 working with Matisse in Collioure and came away with a sense of the other's exceptional personality and manner of painting and of the inner logic of his artistic system. The bright southern light led him to make the staggering discovery that when colours are exceptionally intense, there are no dark shadows and they are full of colour reflexes. In effect Derain came to totally reject shadow as it was. A direct result of this new discovery was the landscape *The Drying Sails*. The burning southern colours and working alongside Matisse revolutionized Derain's way of seeing colour.

In the years 1909-1910 Derain worked a great deal outdoors in the company of Picasso and Braque. *The Castle*, shows the geometrical approach to form which brought Derain so very close to Cubism.. It almost seems as if nature has escaped, torn the artist's control, and is drawing him back to his Mediterranean landscape days. *Grove* and *Tree-Trunks*, were without doubt painted from actual sketches.

It is true that Derain exhibitions were held in Europe and the United States from 1922 right up until the outbreak of the Second World War. However, in Paris, Derain's work was rarely shown after 1916. Derain's work in Russian collections can lay claim to being a definitive representation of the period it covers, because it is a true reflection of one of the most interesting parts of Derain's life, the decade between 1905 and 1914.

It was only in 1910 that Derain, somewhat belatedly, turned his attention to the still-life. Despite possessing a varied and exquisite collection of applied art from all around the world, Derain limited

◄ **André Derain**,
Still Life in Front of the Window, 1912-1913.
Oil on canvas, 128 x 79 cm.
Pushkin State Museum of Fine Arts, Moscow.

his still-life subjects to bottles, clay pitchers, and glazed vases. The still life *Table and Chairs* represents a sort of culmination to Derain's searches in the area of colour and form and is a synthesis of all he gained from Cézanne and from Cubism.

The years 1913-1914 are often termed Derain's "Gothic period." In the still life *View from Window* (1912-1913, Pushkin Museum of Fine Arts), he used exactly the same objects as in previous works, but their meaning is changed in the new context of this composition. The perpendicular window frame which forms the axis of the painting seems to draw the tableware and the trees beyond the window with it in a vertical direction, evoking associations with Gothic church architecture.

Derain, did then, indeed shut himself away from his friends, retiring to his studio and all the African sculptures, Chinese bronzes, Greek terracottas, and Renaissance ceramics that filled it. Later still, he became a hermit, living in his house in Chambourcy. In 1954, on 8 September, Derain died in a car crash.

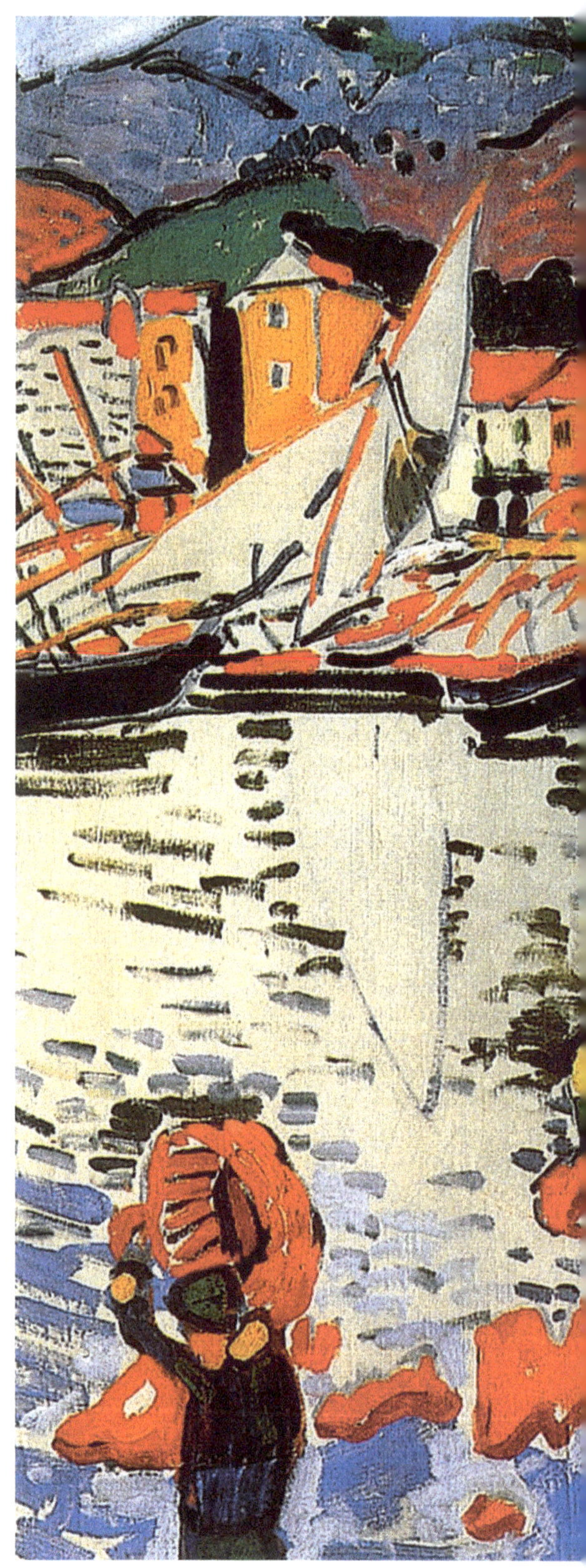

▶ **André Derain**,
Drying the Sails, 1905.
Oil on canvas, 82 x 101 cm.
Pushkin State Museum of Fine Arts, Moscow.

▼ **André Derain**,
Tree-Trunks, 1912-1913.
Oil on canvas, 92 x 73 cm.
Pushkin State Museum of Fine Arts, Moscow. (p. 42)

▼ **André Derain**,
Grove, c. 1912.
Oil on canvas, 116.5 x 81.3 cm.
State Hermitage Museum, Saint Petersburg. (p. 43)

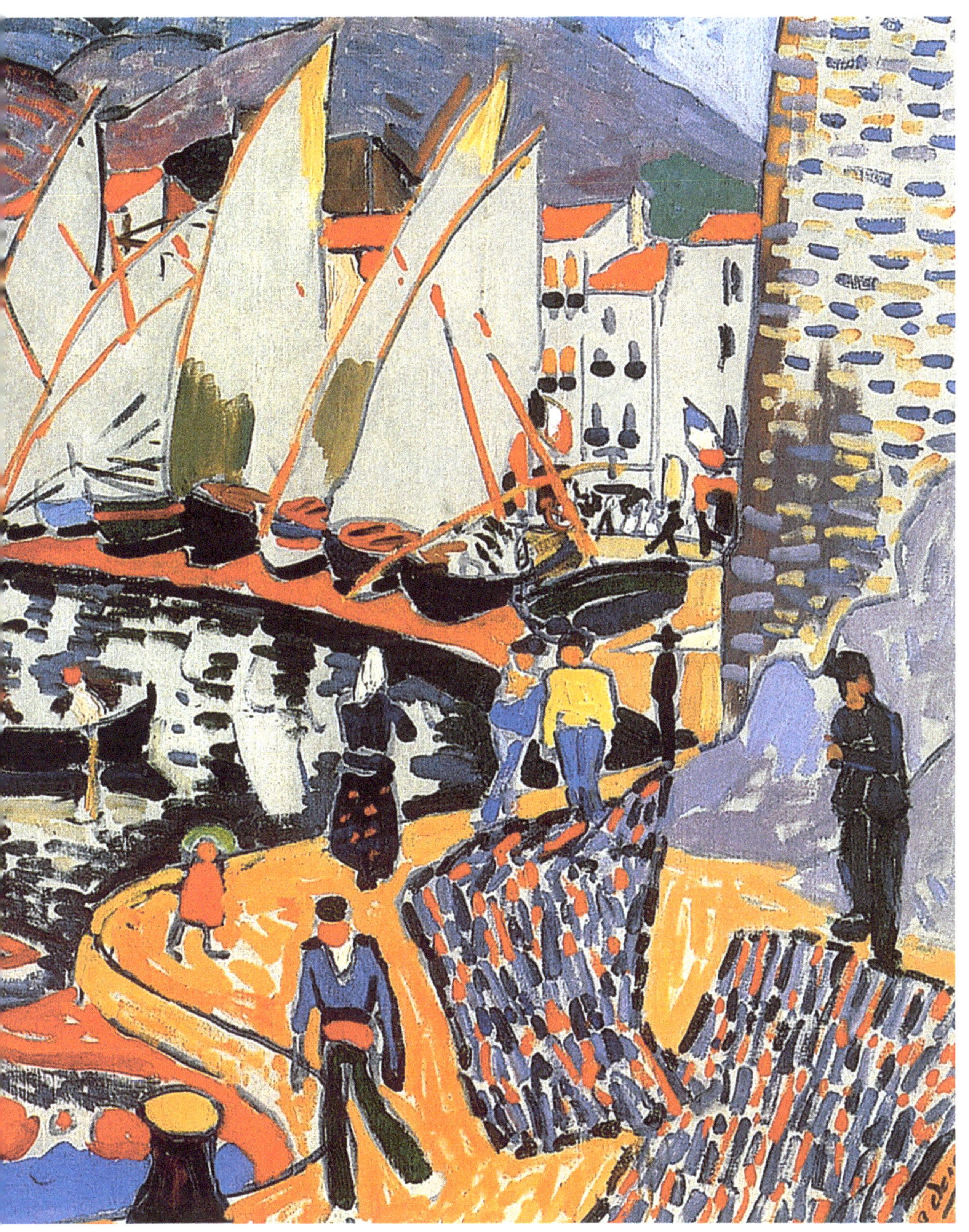

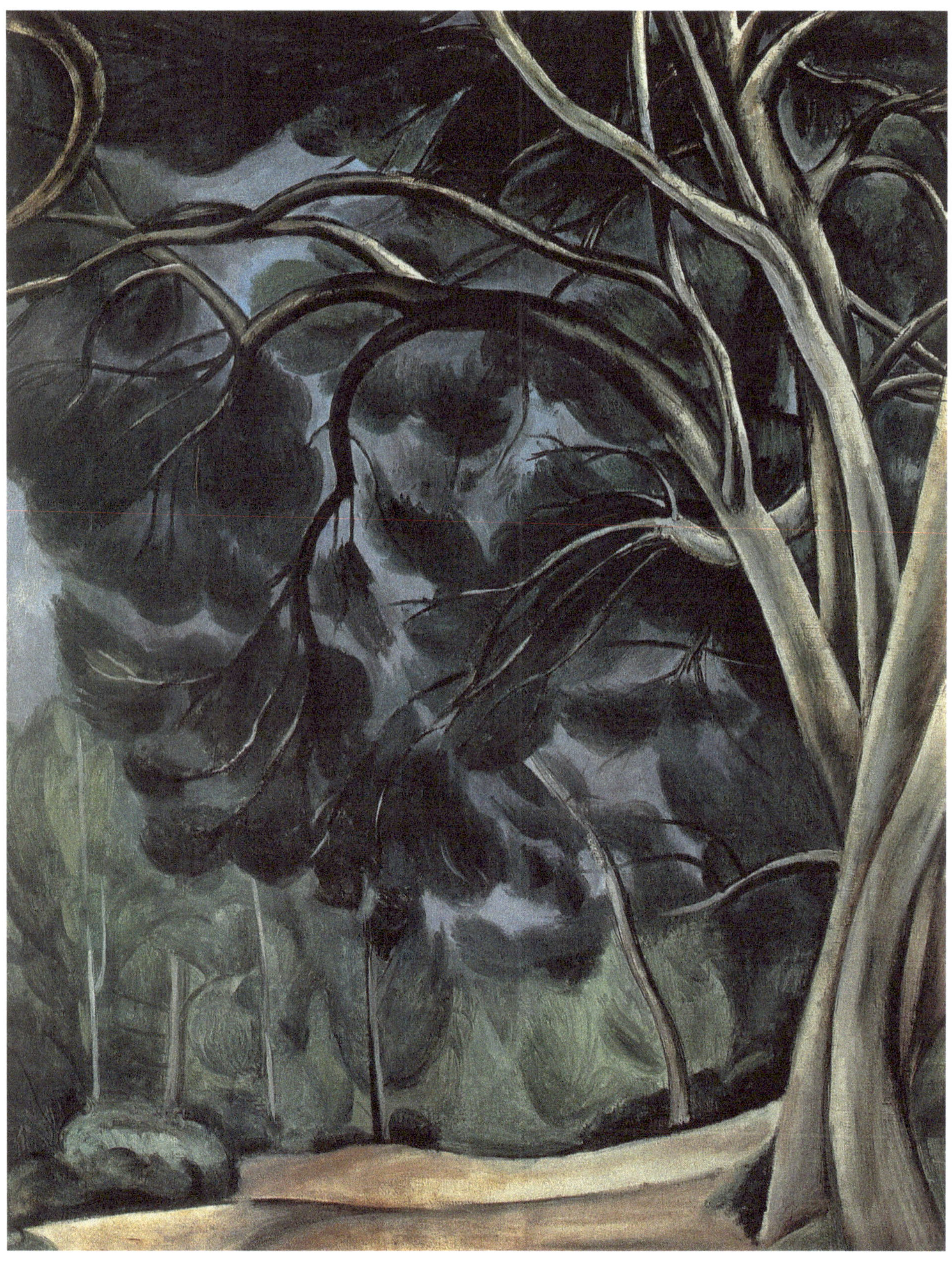

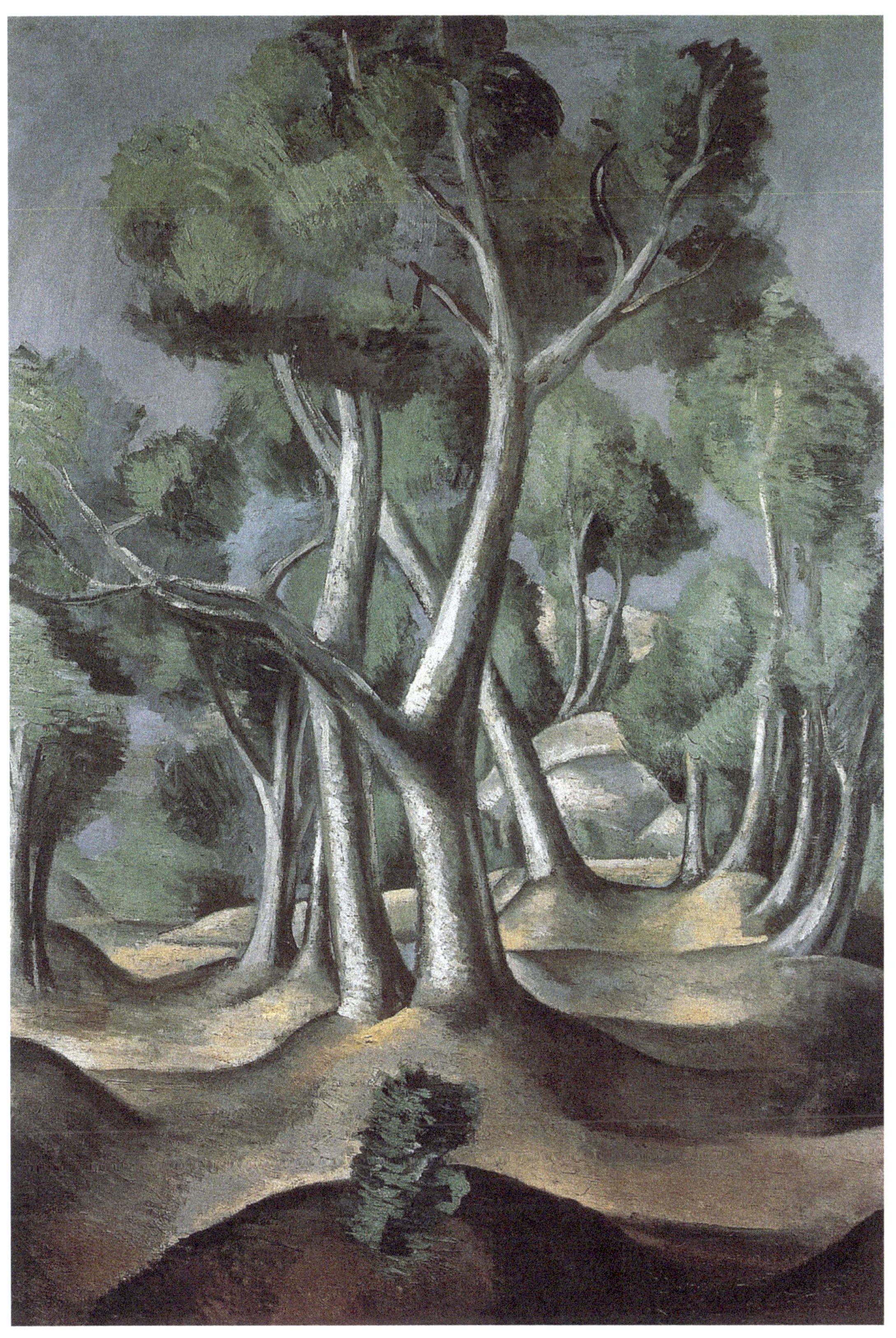

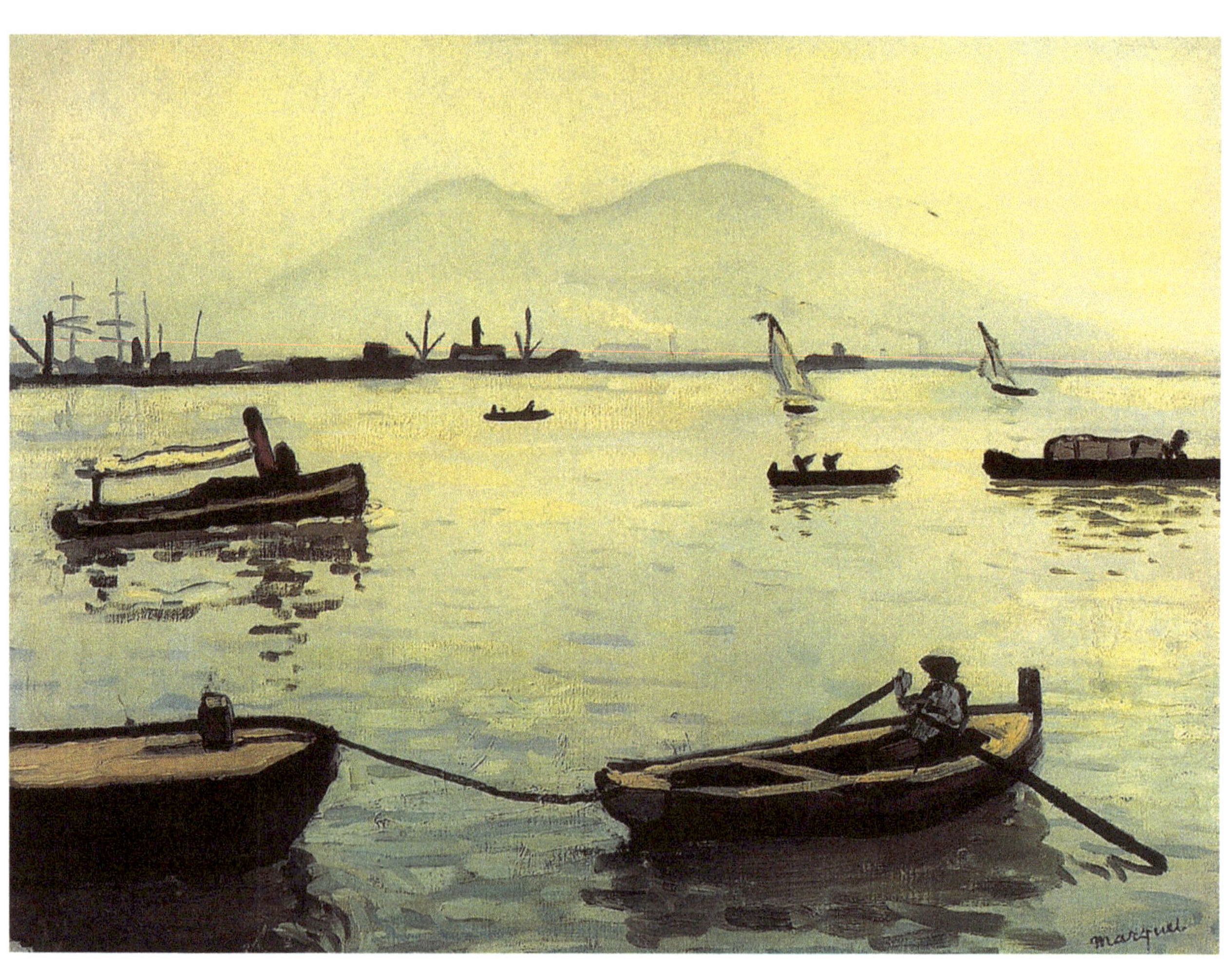
marquet

ALBERT MARQUET

(1875 BORDEAUX – 1947 LA FRETTE-sur-SEINE)

"A Fauve from the very outset, Albert Marquet was also an original Fauve, and moreover, an independent Fauve who in many ways distanced himself from Fauvism." Bernard Dorival wrote those words in 1944. It really is the case that Marquet's painting never possessed the violent energy of Vlaminck and that Matisse's red never rode triumphantly through it. The texture of his painting never displayed that anarchic freedom which also became one of the outward signs of Fauvism.

Albert Marquet was born on 27 March 1875 into the family of a railway clerk in Bordeaux. The taste for drawing which Albert displayed in his childhood and his evident talent prompted his mother to conceive the idea of moving to Paris where he entered, in 1890, the 'École des Arts décoratifs'. It was there that Marquet met Matisse who was six years older than him and for that reason immediately adopted a protective attitude towards him.

◀ **Albert Marquet,**
Vesuvius, c. 1909.
Oil on canvas, 61 x 80 cm.
Pushkin State Museum of Fine Arts, Moscow.

Professor Gustave Moreau called Marquet "mon ennemi intime" [my intimate enemy], an epithet which expressed both his inability to overcome Marquet's stubborn spirit of contradiction and his fondness for this pupil. Marquet had a reverence for the professor, as they all did, but his acute and specific gift as a draughtsman irresistibly distracted him away from academic lessons and the copying of the classics which Moreau so insistently preached, towards living scenes of the life he saw in the street.

By now, though, he was already a professionally mature artist and he presented his works in several places: In 1903 at Berthe Weill and at the 1905 'Salon d'Automne ' where Marquet was among the few about whom the critics wrote in completely favourable terms. Marquet's painting never outraged either the critics or the public. Nevertheless, the epithet "Fauve" suited Marquet as naturally as everything he did throughout a life in which he stood by the creative principle and bonds of friendship forged at the beginning of the century.

The landscape *The Quai du Louvre* (c. 1907, Pushkin Museum of Fine Arts) was painted at the time of the Fauves most striking public

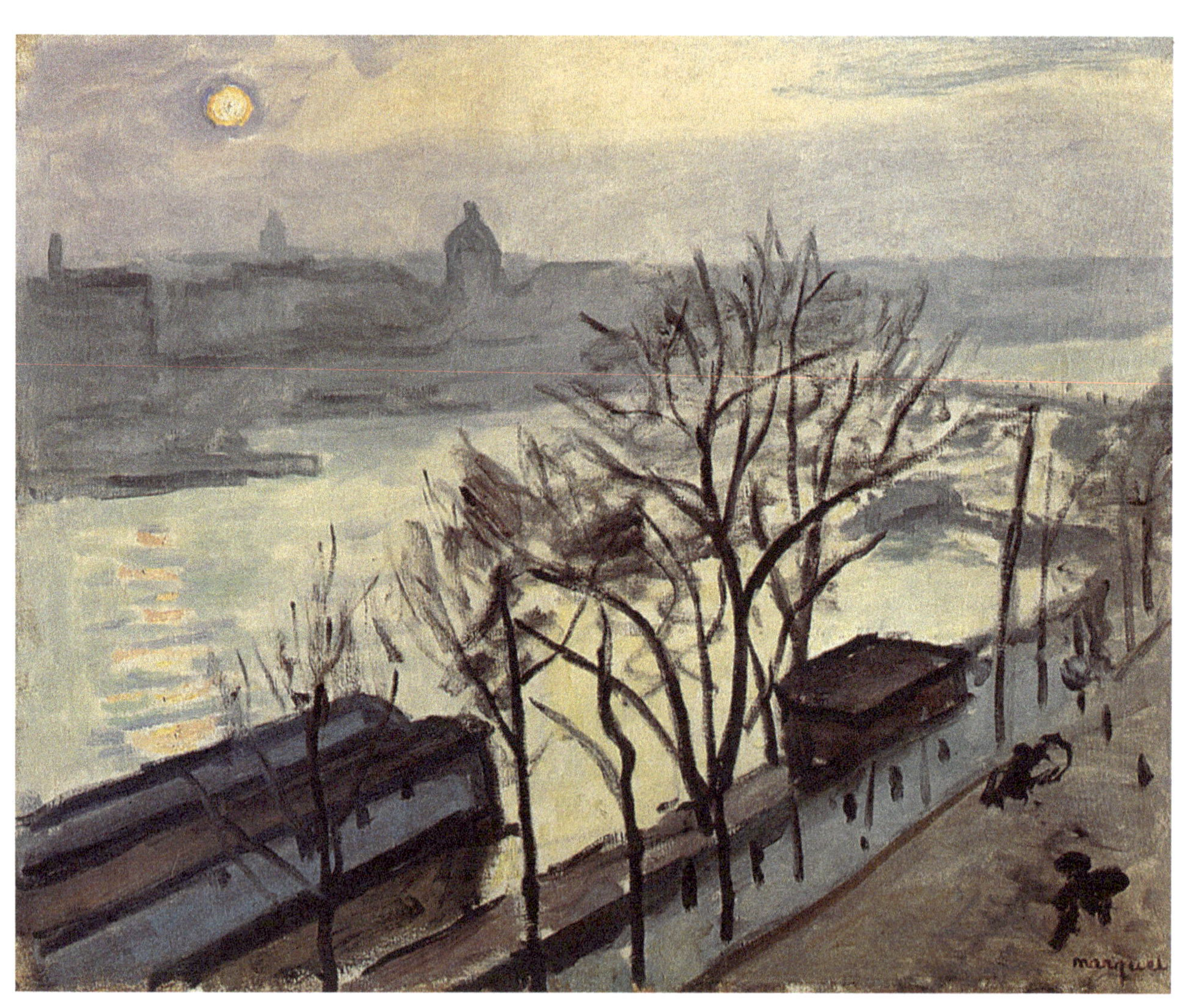

▲ **Albert Marquet**,
Sun Over Paris (Sun Seen Through the Trees), c. 1910.
Oil on canvas, 65 x 89 cm.
Pushkin State Museum of Fine Arts, Moscow.

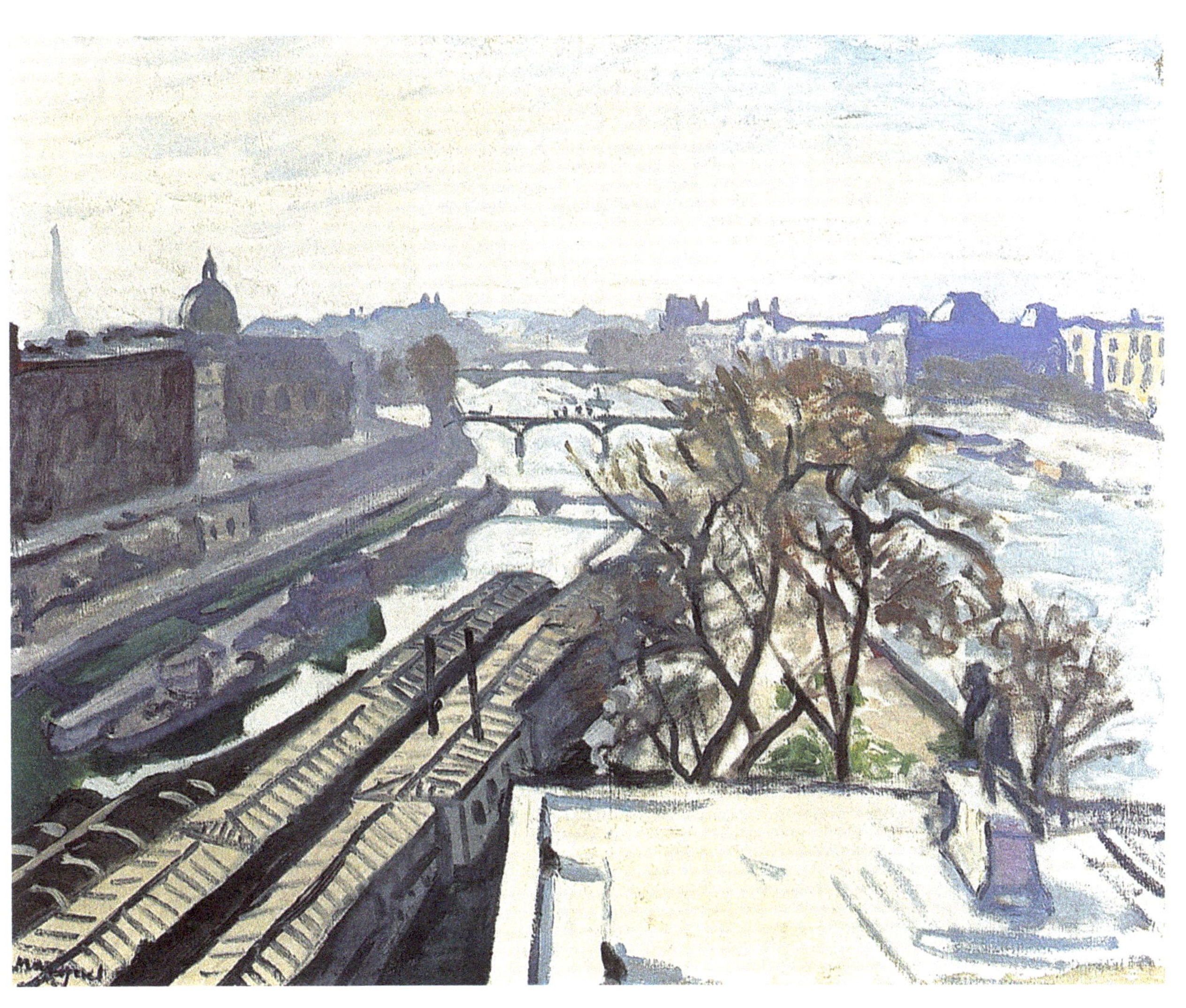

▲ **Albert Marquet**,
View of the Seine and the Monument to Henri IV, c. 1906.
Oil on canvas, 65.5 x 81 cm.
State Hermitage Museum, Saint Petersburg.

demonstrations. The red colour appears here only in the form of a few horizontal strokes in the reflection of the sun, but they too grow dim on the whitish water. In the years that followed, Marquet exhibited jointly with other Fauves in Brussels, Vienna, and Prague. For the majority of the Fauves, landscape was of primary importance and in Marquet's case it became virtually the only genre in his painting. On rare occasions he turned his hand to the nude, the portrait, and the still life.

While he had a warm affection and respect for Paul Signac, Neo-Impressionism never influenced him for a moment; Cézanne impressed him no less than the others, yet he did not become a Cézannist. Marquet created his own brand of landscape in his painting and it was in that fact above all that his natural affinity with Fauvism expressed itself. In the accomplishment of the task, which Manguin held to be the main one for the Fauves – the intensification of light in painting – it was Marquet who probably played the main role. Marquet's world fitted smoothly into the general picture of Fauvism – without the work of any one of the "trio" (Matisse, Marquet, and Manguin) that picture would not only be incomplete, but would fail to reflect all aspects of a many-sided phenomenon.

The Mediterranean landscapes *Harbour at Menton* (1905) and View of Saint-Jean-de-Luz were painted in keeping with the Fauvist colourist tendency. But in order to unite sea and sky with a blinding pure shade of pale blue, Marquet needed the southern sun, something without which Vlaminck managed perfectly well when depicting the bright blue in his *Barge on the Seine*.

Like Matisse, Marquet was exempted from military service, and he spent the years of the First World War in the south of France. He worked in Collioure, the Estaque range and in Marseilles, where, in 1916, a friend let Marquet have a comfortable studio in which he established himself for a period of three years. His contract with Druet meant that he did not have to worry about money.

In 1920 Marquet set off for Algeria, his decision backed by the advice of doctors who recommended that after a severe bout of influenza, he spent the winter in southern climes rather than in Paris. One of the letters of recommendation with which Marquet's friends furnished him was addressed to Marcelle Martinet, a French woman who lived in Algeria who helped him to discover and experience the life of the Arabic world and whom he married in 1923. Marquet and his wife then spent their time between Paris and Alger, as well as travelling widely. In 1945 the couple returned to the apartment at I Rue Dauphine. It was there that the artist died on 14 June 1947.

▶ **Albert Marquet**,
View of Saint-Jean-de-Luz, 1907.
Oil on canvas, 60 x 81 cm.
State Hermitage Museum, Saint Petersburg.

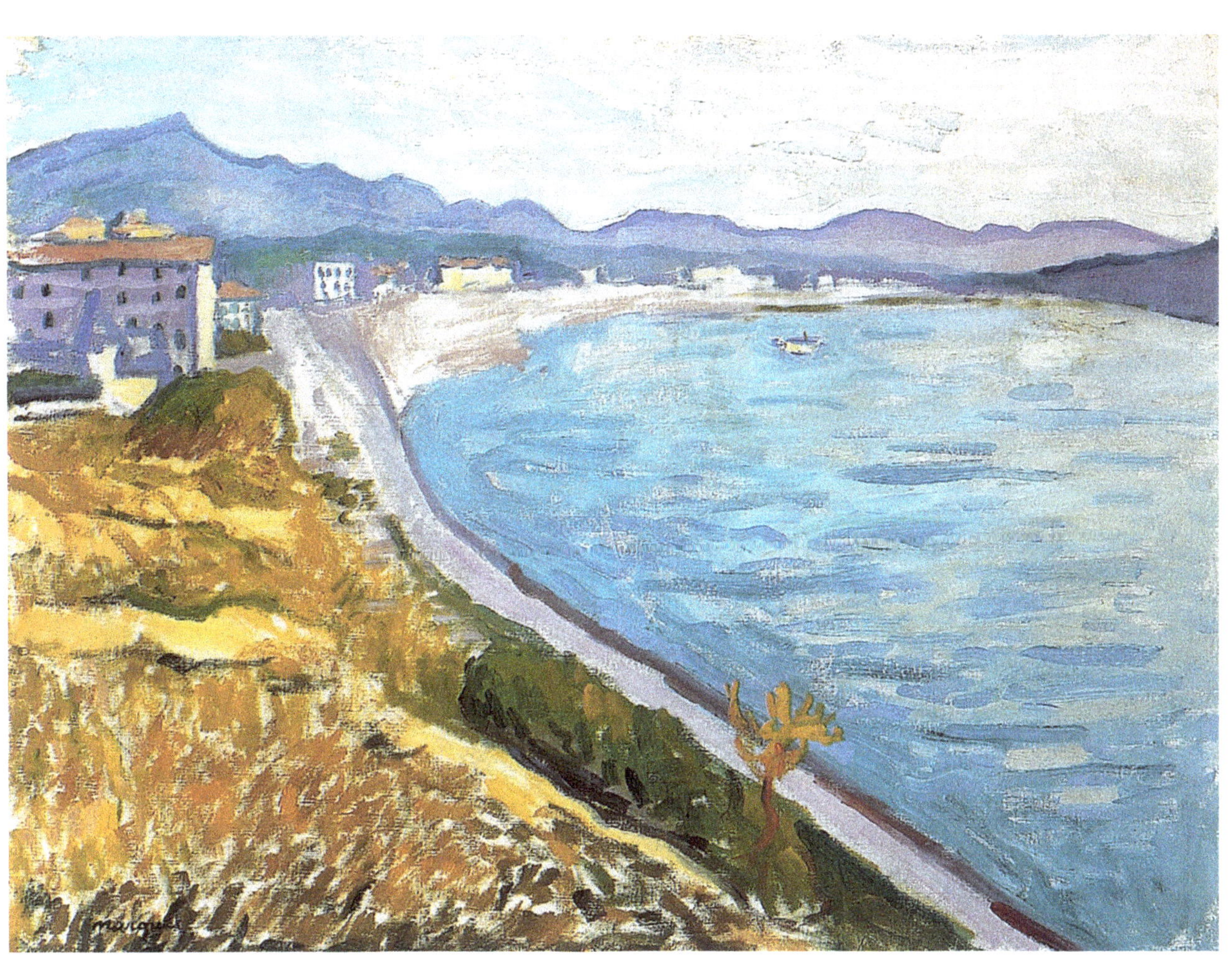

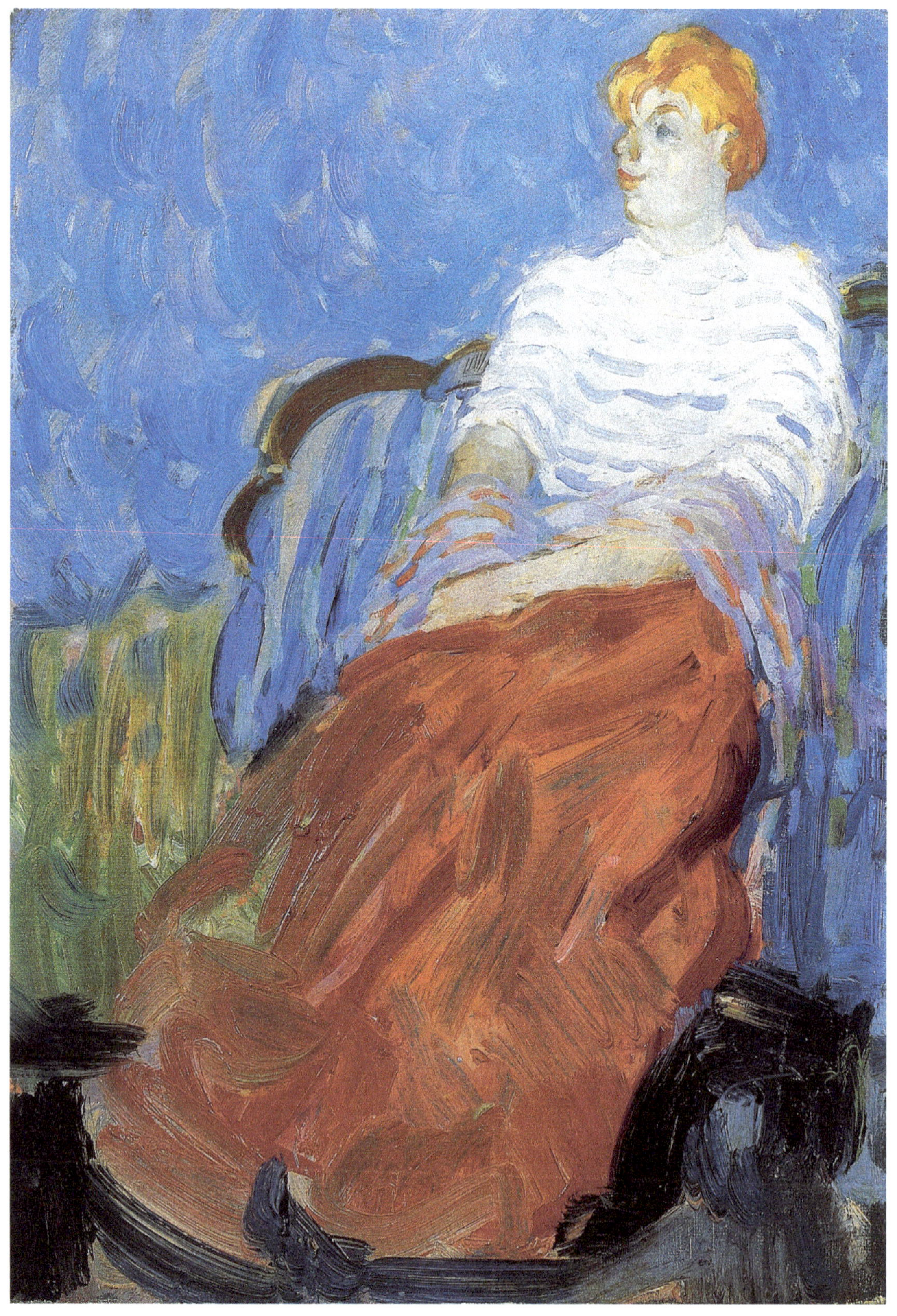

RAOUL DUFY

(1877 LE HAVRE – 1953 FORCALQUIER)

Maurice de Vlaminck, the "wildest" of the Fauves, was enraptured by Dufy: "The work of Raoul Dufy is more unquestionable and more original than that of Henri Matisse. Dufy is not tempted like Matisse by the solution of plastic problems. He quite simply thinks of his painting. Like the palm reader who uses the lines on a woman's hand to discover her character, Raoul Dufy uses the lines of his drawing to convey his vision of things, to describe the gestures and motion of what he sees living and stirring....."

Dufy was close to Vlaminck in the absolute freedom of his painting and like Vlaminck, he loved flowers, trees, birds, and butterflies. Dufy did not resemble anyone else. He made contact with his future-Fauvist friends in 1900 precisely because at the age of twenty-three, he possessed the same qualities. Just like the other Fauves, he was opposed on principle to theories and groupings; like all of them, to the end of his life he valued the friendship and preserved the attachments of his youth. At the same time as his friends, Dufy became carried away by the lessons of Cézanne and made tentative steps in Cubism under the influence of his friend and Montmartre neighbour, Pablo Picasso. Like the majority of the Fauves, Dufy then rejected that course.

◄ **Raoul Dufy**,
Portrait of Suzanne Dufy, the Artist's Sister, 1904.
Oil on canvas, 46 x 33 cm.
State Hermitage Museum, Saint Petersburg.

Raoul Dufy was born in Le Havre on 3 June 1877. One of nine children in the family, he retained a love of music all his life. At the age of fifteen he had to go out and earn his living. His work for a Swiss coffee merchant's firm was connected with the sea and ships which he drew and painted in his leisure hours. In 1900, after he had done his military service, Dufy was awarded a grant to study art at the 'École des Beaux-art's in Paris. In 1901 Dufy exhibited one painting at the 'Salon des Artistes Français'; in 1902 he sold his first pastel to Berthe Weill; from 1903 onwards he exhibited at the 'Salon des Indépendants 'and at group exhibitions in the Galery Berthe Weill.

It was no mere chance that Dufy produced his own *Bal du Moulin de la Galette* – the artist had a need to say a similar thing, but in his own, different language. *Woman Seated* (1904, Hermitage) also comes across as a personal reworking of a motif by Renoir. The fascination of the living world gives way to a light-hearted grotesque thanks to the artist's decorative imagination.

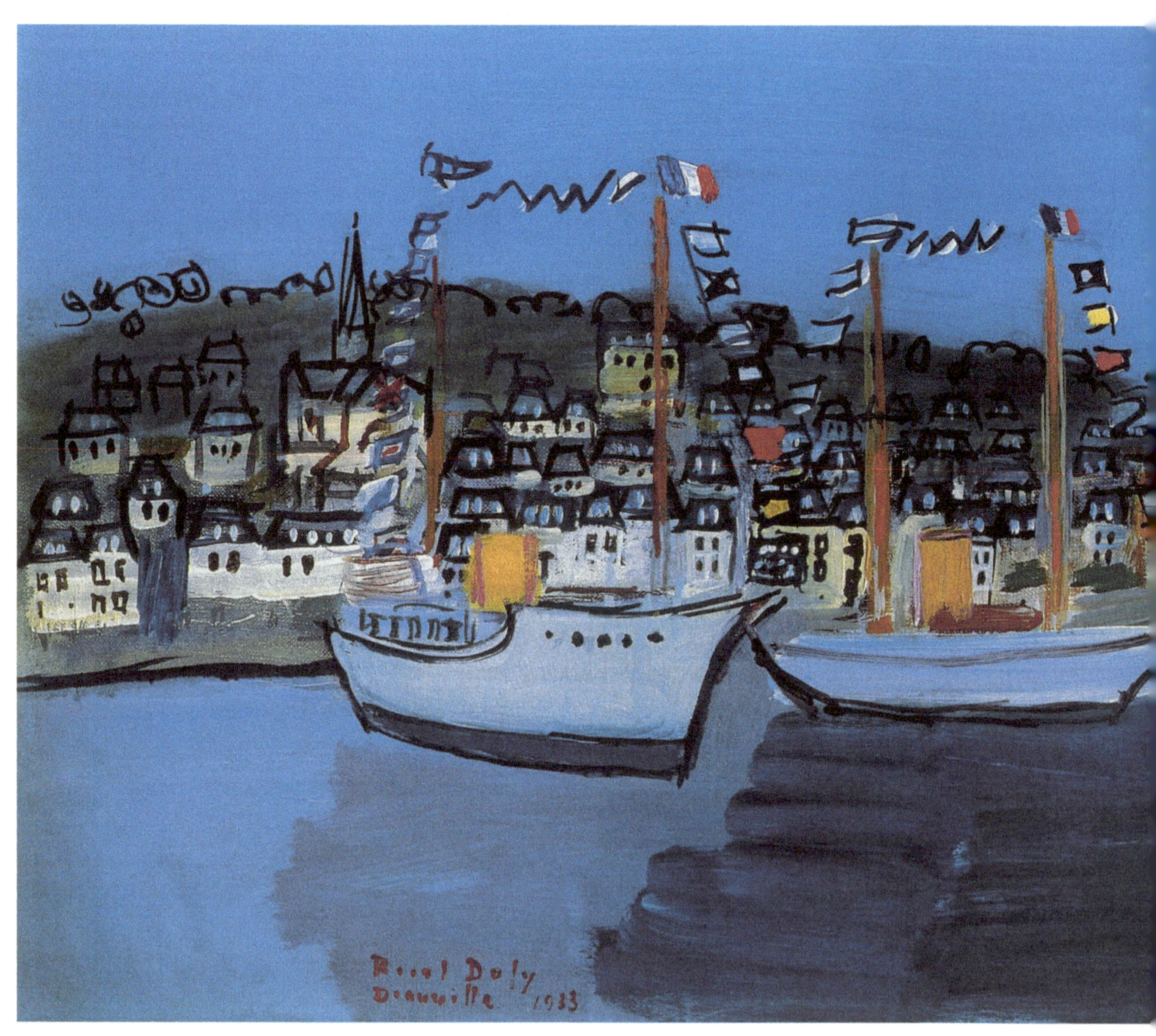

▲ **Raoul Dufy,**
14 July in Deauville, 1933.
Oil on canvas, 38 x 92 cm.
Pushkin State Museum of Fine Arts, Moscow.

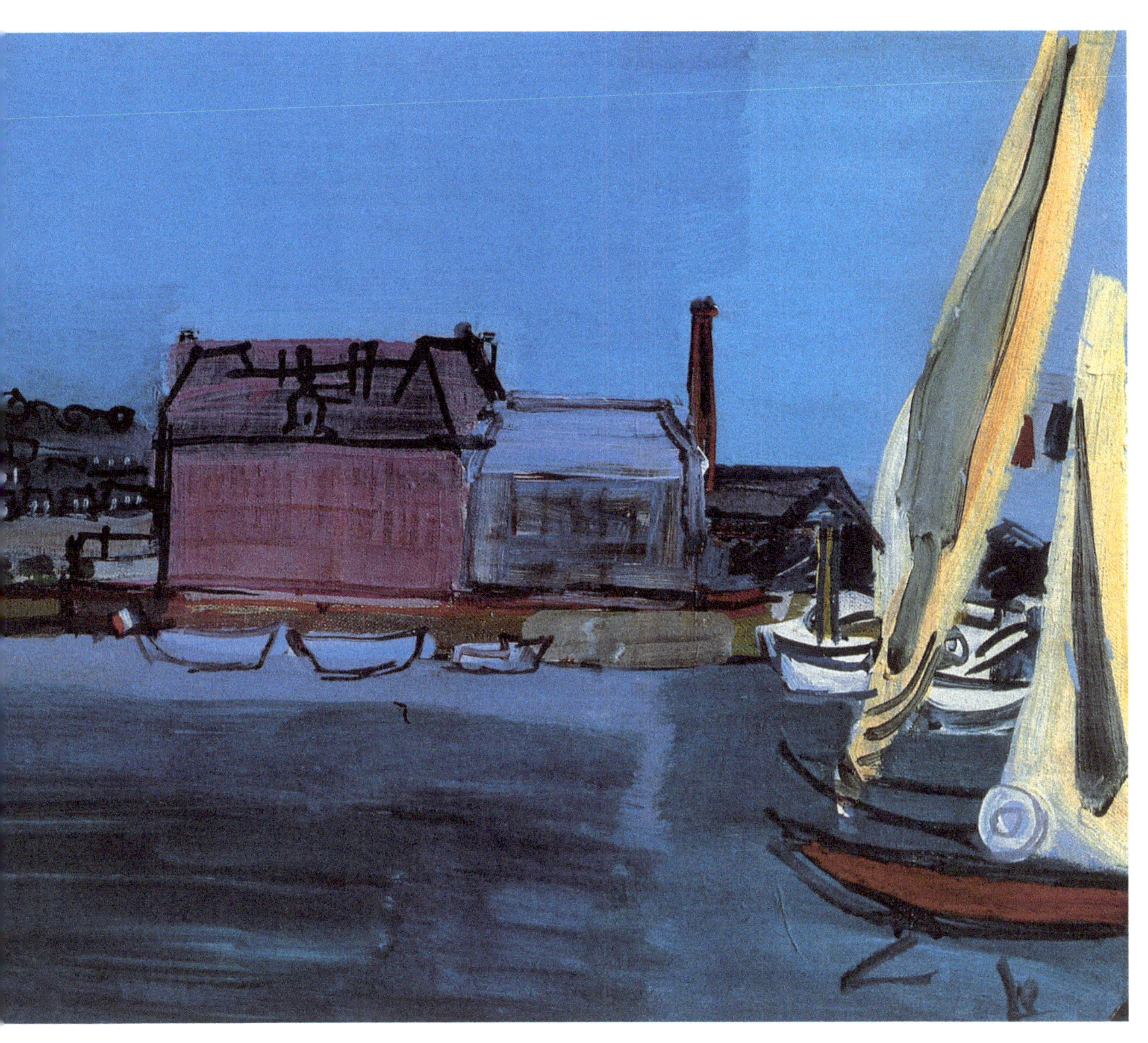

▼ **Raoul Dufy,**
The Antibes, 1926.
Gouache and watercolour on paper, 50.6 x 65.5 cm.
Pushkin State Museum of Fine Arts,
Moscow. (pp. 54-55)

In 1905 Dufy displayed his work at the 'Salon des Indépendants 'and at the 'Salon d'Automne ' where he earned himself the name of Fauve together with the others. In 1906, Berthe Weill organized his first one-man exhibition. During this period, Dufy settled on Montmartre, opposite the 'Bateau Lavoir', in a studio which Friesz had given up in his favour. In 1908 Dufy worked at 'l'Estaque' together with Georges Braque;

The second painting by Dufy, *14 July at Deauville*, was donated to the Moscow museum in 1969 by the collector M. Kaganovitch, in whose Paris gallery a Dufy exhibition was held in 1936. A favourite motif of Dufy's since childhood – the Normandy coast, the sea and ships – is painted in the landscape format often used by the artist. This painting is a concentration of many things: Dufy's attitude to the natural world and to colour, the poetic nature of his painting, decorativeness, and, most importantly, the feeling of joy which radiates from all his work.

A series of his exhibitions toured Europe and America before and during the Second World War when Dufy moved to the south of France, away from the German occupation. Even then, Dufy was receiving treatment for arthritis which plagued him as it had Renoir, an artist of whom he was especially fond. In 1951 Dufy produced his own version of Renoir's composition *Bal du Moulin de la Galette* (1876, Musée d'Orsay, Paris) in an almost symbolic gesture: tormented but not broken by the illness, Dufy – like Renoir – managed to invest his painting with joy right up to the end. Dufy died on 23 March 1953 in Forcalquier.

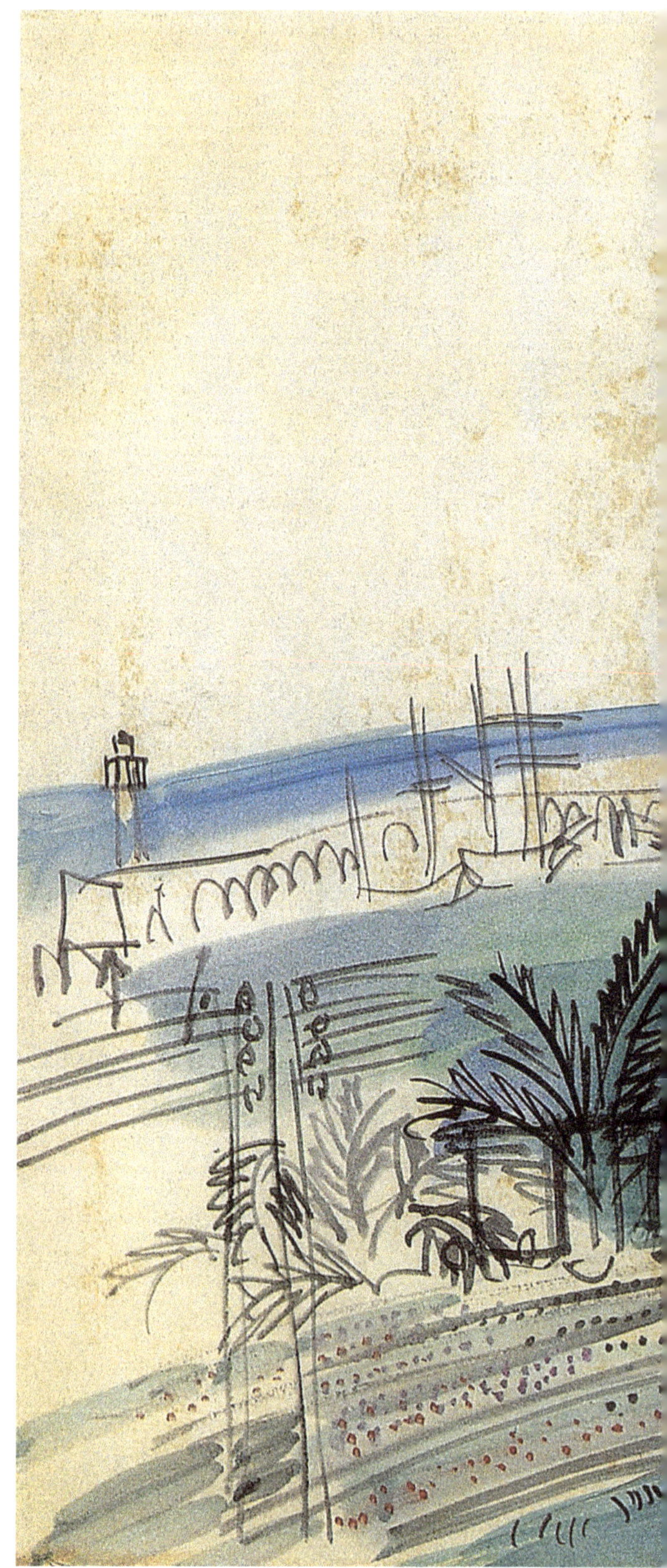

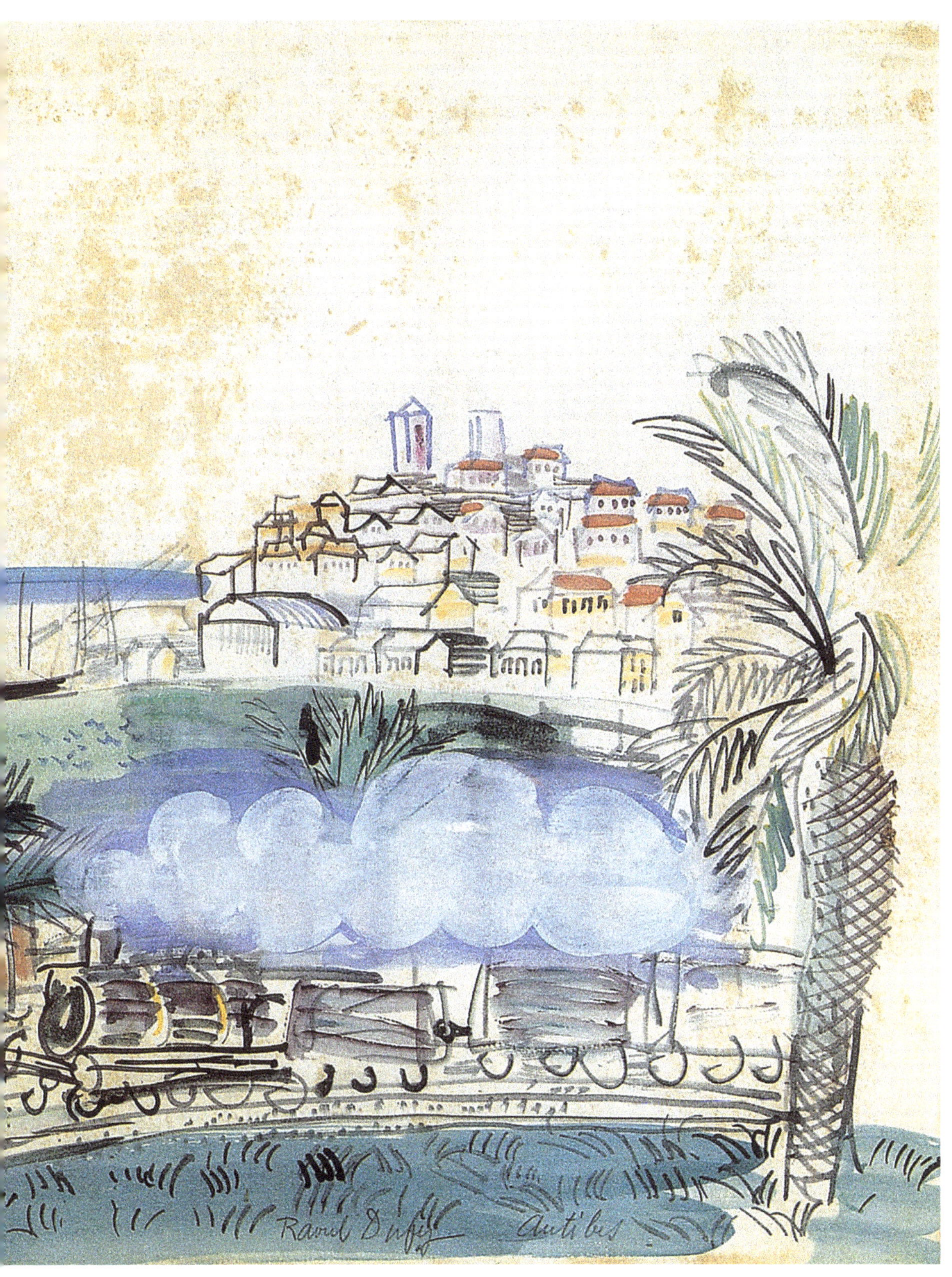
Raoul Dufy
Antibes

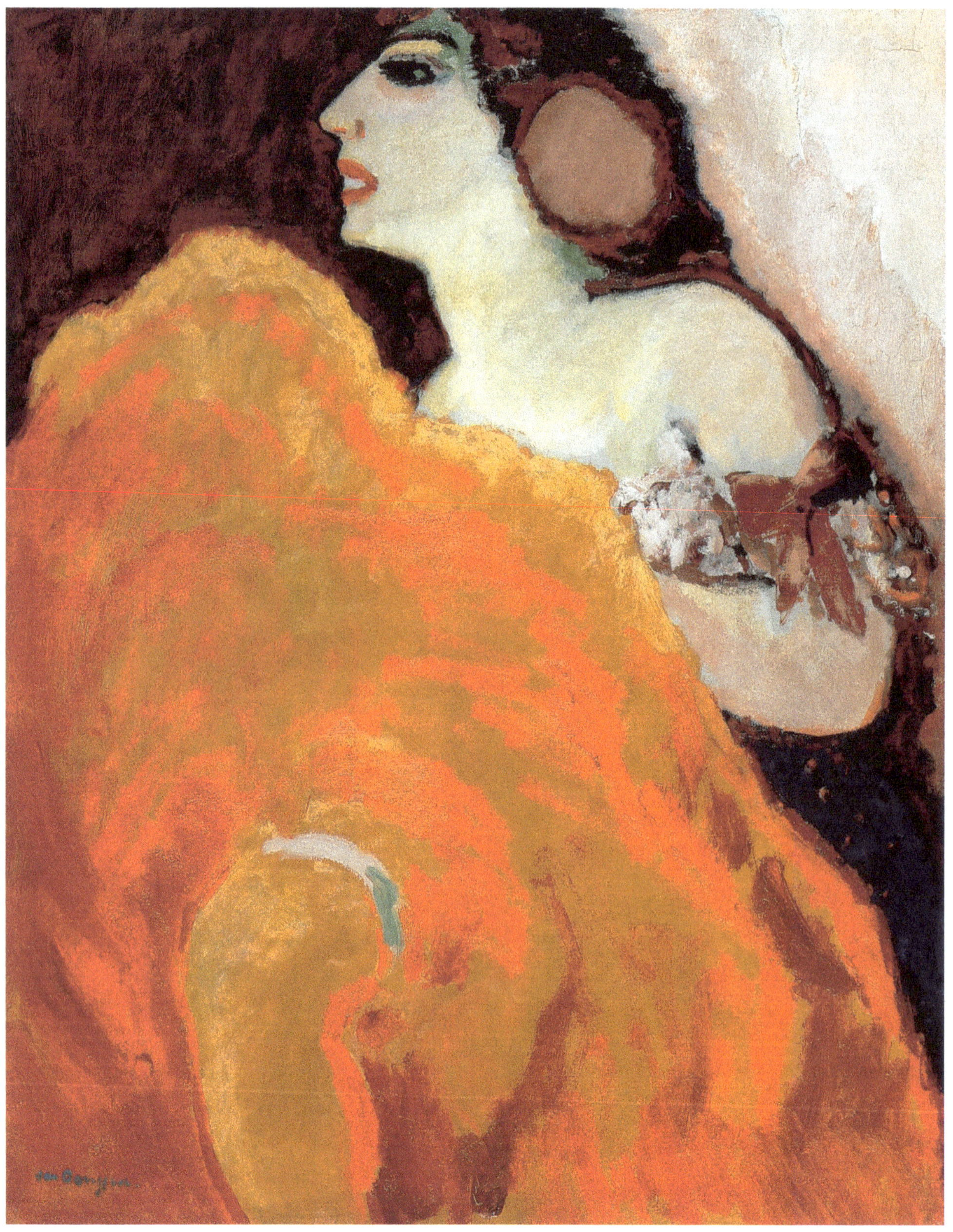

KEES VAN DONGEN

(1877 AMSTERDAM – 1968 MONTE CARLO)

"The Fauvist bomb was a fabrication made up by the litterateurs, and it only became a bomb after fifty years of recollections. At the time it was at most a petard." Van Dongen's irony was part of his artistic means and at the same time a means of self-defence. In his attempt to divide Van Dongen's work up into periods, his main biographer, Louis Chaumeil, distinguishes a "period of Fauvism" and, extending through all the following years, a "worldly period," the name of which is not connected to any particular stylistic peculiarity for the very reason that Van Dongen's art belonged entirely to Fauvism.

◄ **Kees van Dongen**,
The Red Dancer, 1907.
Oil on canvas, 99.7 x 81 cm.
State Hermitage Museum, Saint Petersburg.

▼ **Kees Van Dongen**,
Spanish Woman, 1910-1911.
Oil on canvas, 46 x 39 cm.
Pushkin State Museum of Fine Arts, Moscow. (p. 58)

▼ **Kees Van Dongen**,
Antonia La Coquinera, 1906.
Oil on canvas, 100 x 81 cm.
State Hermitage Museum, Saint Petersburg. (p. 59)

Kees (Cornelis Theodore Maria) van Dongen was born into the family of a Dutch brewer living in Delfshaven, a suburb of Rotterdam, on 26 January 1877. In Holland he obtained a professional training, studying for four years at the Royal Academy of Fine Arts in Rotterdam. In 1897 he used money his father gave him to take a tourist trip to Paris for the Bastille Day holiday. "Paris drew me like a beacon," he confessed later.

After that, came a period spent back in Holland. It wasn't until 1899 that Van Dongen settled in Paris with his wife, the artist, Augusta Preitinger. At this time in Montmartre he made the acquaintance of other anarchists as young and bold as himself – the future Fauves. As 1905 was essential to all of the Fauves, it was a landmark in Van Dongen's life, as well. Van Dongen submitted only two paintings for the famous 'Salon d'Automne' because a personal exhibition of his work had been arranged for the same time at the Galerie Druet.

The art business was fairly profitable, making it now possible for Van Dongen to travel. Spain and Morocco drew him with their aspect of the exotic which he was always inclined to seek

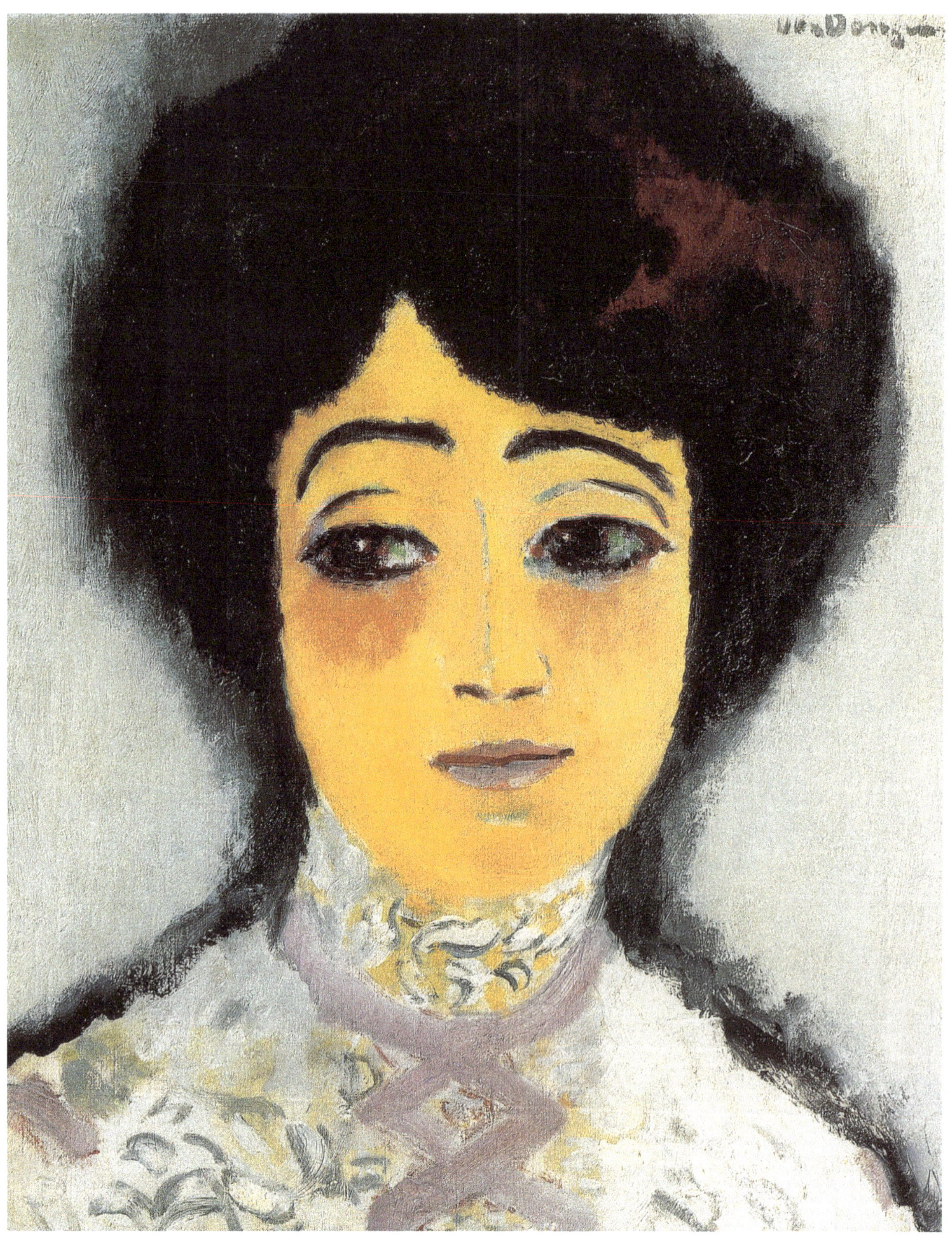

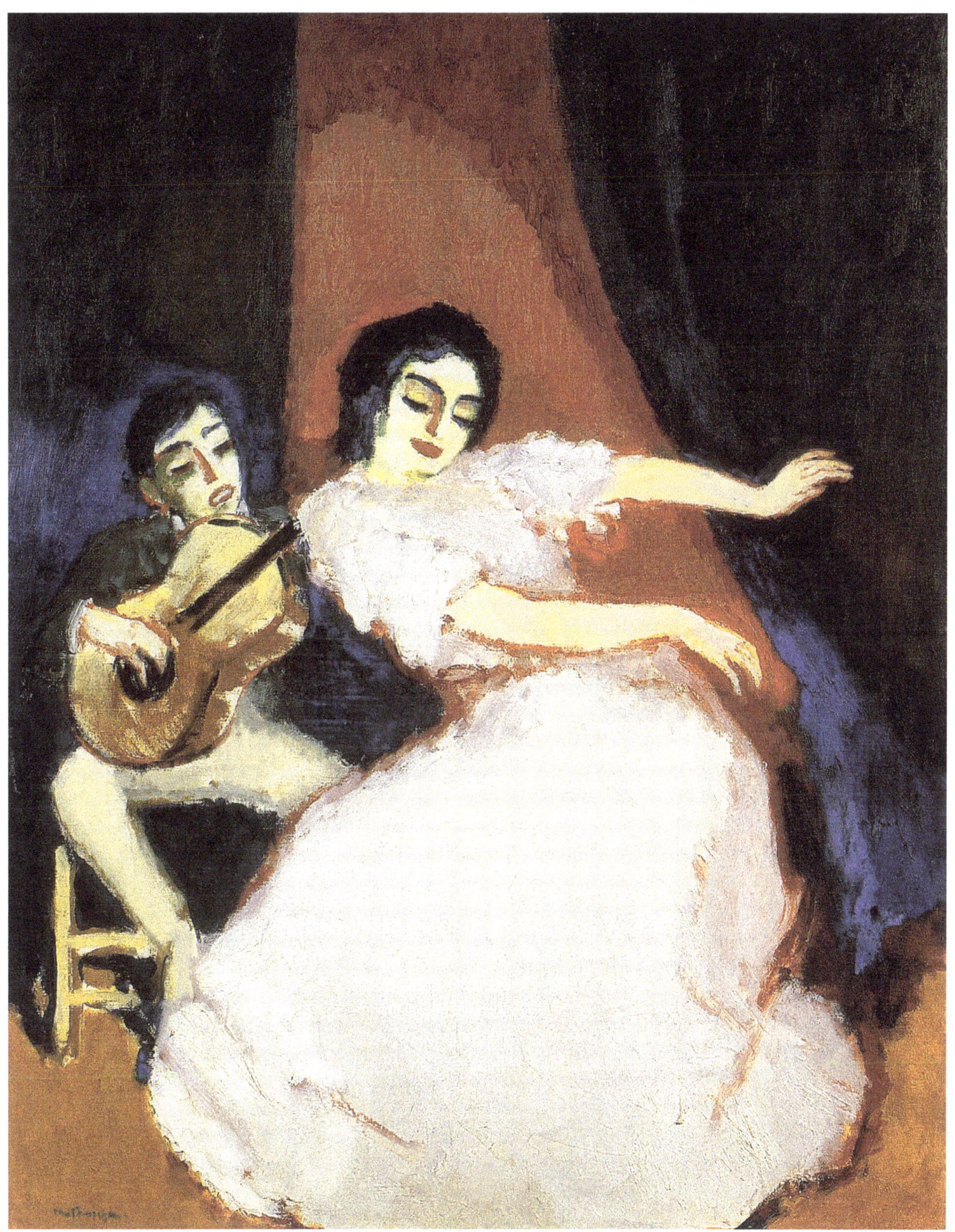

out. Something new appeared in his manner of painting – refined, elongated lines, a tendency towards the grotesque. There was a glaring contradiction between his worldly success and the way he created his portraits in a manner sometimes bordering on the grotesque which he retained to the end of his days.

Lady in a Black Hat was a continuation, as it were, of Van Dongen's reflections on beauty – this is one more aspect of it, that splendid image which, in Van Dongen's words, is not a photograph of life but belongs to the realm of the daydream. The wide-brimmed hat and green raincoat give the model a timeless character, taking us away from the sphere of observed life. The mass of green, just like the large black patch of the hat, are present on the canvas so as to cause the warm pink tones of the face with its huge dark eyes to light up tenderly. It is hard to consider *The Spanish Woman* (1910-1911, Pushkin Museum of Fine Arts) a portrait, although the features are distinctive and clearly drawn from life. On a grey background, unusually flat for Van Dongen, an orange-golden face shines out, modelled in colour in a barely detectable way. A geometrical ornament appears on the grey dress – a hint of the future arabesque.

The appearance of such paintings was a result of the impressions Van Dongen gained on his first visit to Spain. At the same time as those canvases of 1906-1908 which were full of motion and spatially elaborate, he was also painting works like *Spring* (1907-1908, Hermitage). Spring is reminiscent of the depiction of fruit trees in the work of the Dutch artist Piet Mondrian for whom they became the foundation for a gradual geometrization of design and simplification of colour. The exquisite lines of the branches fan out, becoming the graphic skeleton of the painting. Strung on these are several horizontal arched rows of patches of colour: greens, pinks, whites, and light blues.

In 1929 he took French citizenship, thus reinforcing his position as "the Parisian Dutchman." Soon after, in 1931 he organized the exhibition Trente Années de l'Art in his own studio. From the 1930s his paintings were exhibited in America, Belgium, Holland, Britain, and Switzerland. In 1967 a major retrospective exhibition was held first in Paris and then in Rotterdam to mark the artist's ninetieth birthday. Van Dongen died in Monte Carlo on 27 May 1968.

▶ **Kees van Dongen**,
Woman in a Black Hat, 1908.
Oil on canvas, 100 x 81.5 cm.
State Hermitage Museum, Saint Petersburg.

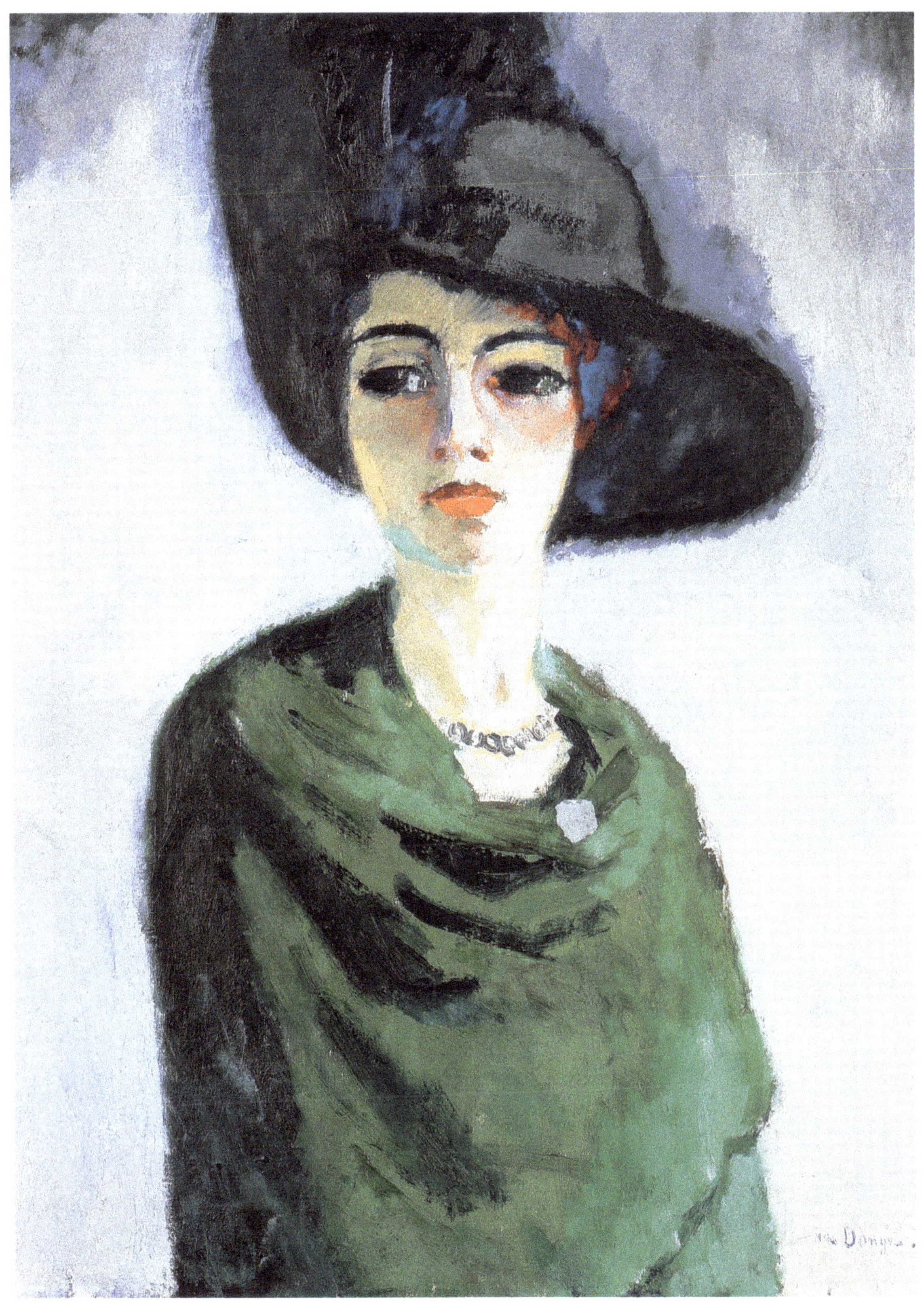

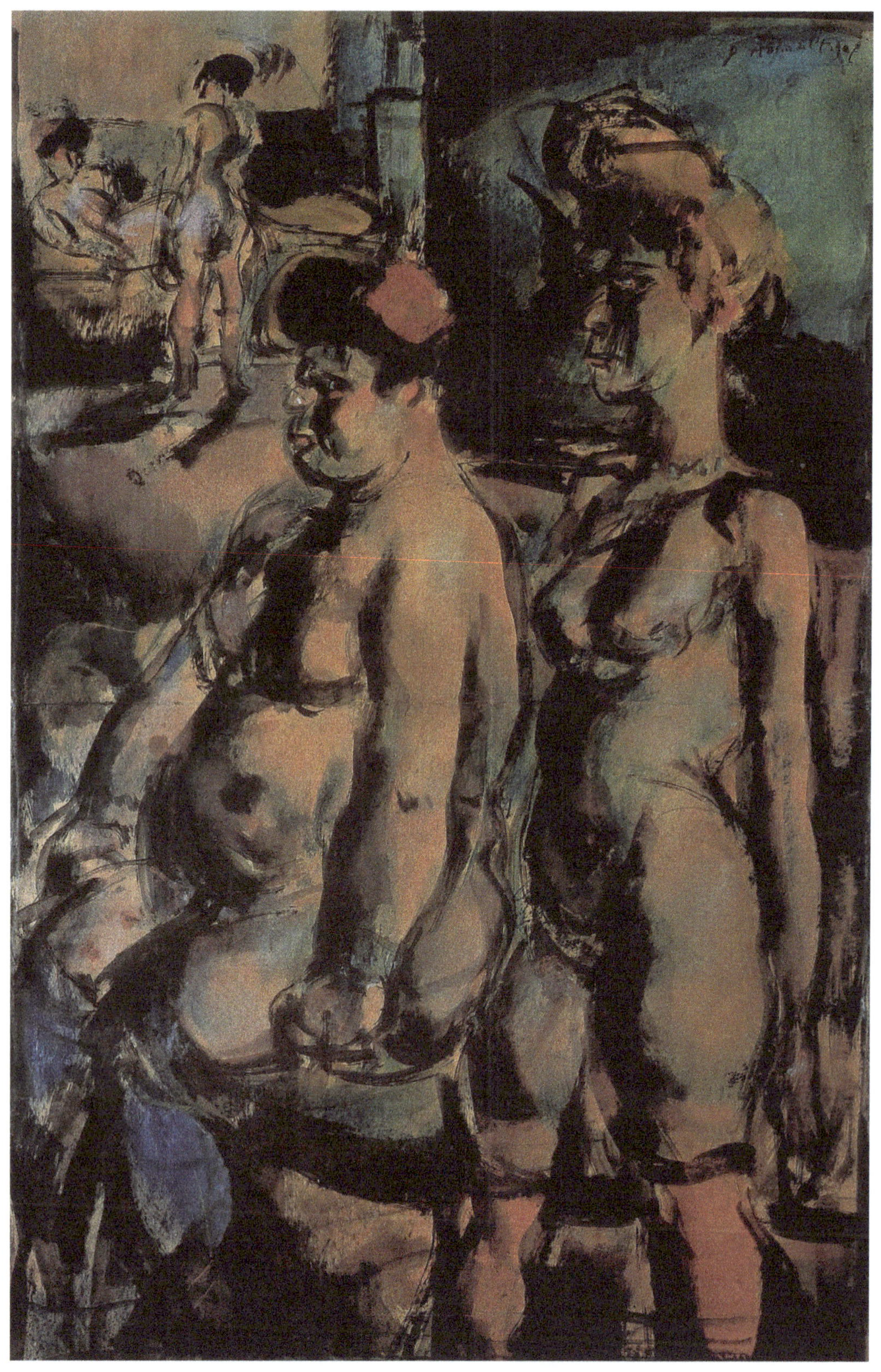

GEORGES ROUAULT

(1871 - 1958 PARIS)

Andre Salmon, the poet and chronicler of Montmartre life, in striving to attribute a unique role to each of the figures of the artistic avant-garde dubbed Georges Rouault "un Fauve d'Apocalypse." There cannot be the slightest doubt about the genuineness of Rouault's Fauvism – he was one of Gustave Moreau's pupils and active alongside Matisse not only at the beginning of their appearances as a group, but also at the foundation of the 'Salon d'Automne ' itself. No less energetically than Vlaminck, Rouault asserted his right to that very freedom and subjectivity in art which was one of the most important characteristics of Fauvism.

It is possible to assert that Rouault was just as indispensable a member of the Fauve community as Maurice de Vlaminck or Kees van Dongen was. His talent with its unique quality acted as a counterweight to the other Fauves' obsession with colour which sets him quite distinctly apart within the Fauvist circle and evokes doubts about the genuineness of his kind of Fauvism – which led to Dorival coining his formula. Doubts of this kind can probably only be justified by a narrow conception of Fauvism, as covering a period of no more than a few years and defined exclusively by the primacy of colour.

◄ **Georges Rouault**,
Les Filles (The Girls), 1907.
Pastel and tempera on paper, 97 x 65 cm.
State Hermitage Museum, Saint Petersburg.

Georges Rouault was born on 27 May 1871 at the height of the battles over the Paris Commune in a cellar where his family had taken refuge from the shooting. His mother's father was a passionate admirer of Honoré Daumier and Édouard Manet. The story has come down that his grandfather, expecting to find only sorrow in the destroyed house and learning instead of the child's arrival, declared: "Perhaps he will be an artist."

Rouault began his artistic career in the crafts when his father apprenticed him to the stained-glass maker Albert Besnard. He achieved such progress in this field that the artist suggested he produce some stained-glass panels to his designs. Yet Rouault longed for the fine arts. At the same time as he was working with stained-glass he attended evening courses at the 'École des Arts décoratifs' and in 1890 he entered the École des Beaux-Arts to study under Professor Elie Delaunay. His embarkation upon the independent course of the artistic avant-garde was entirely natural. In 1903 he was among

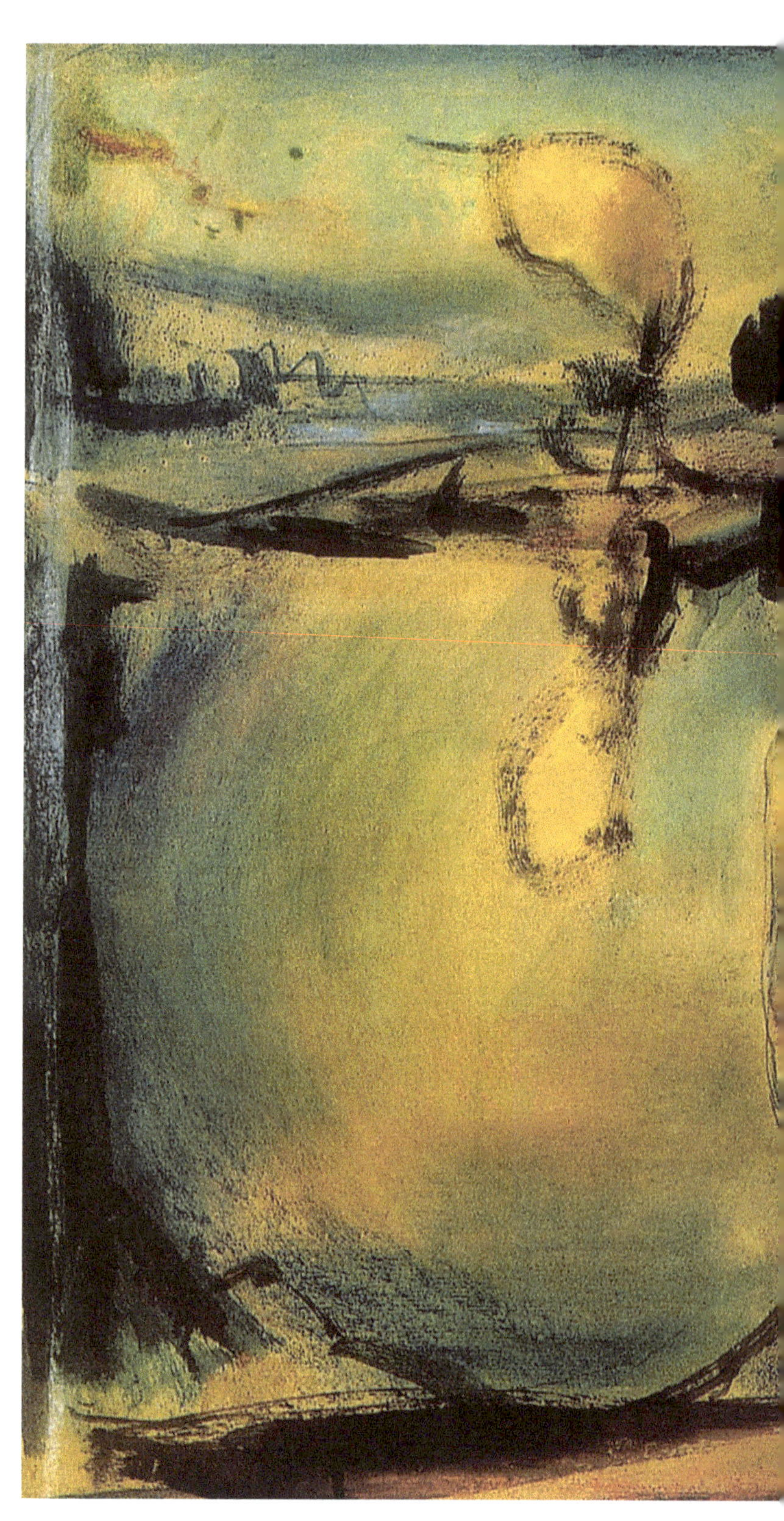

▶ **Georges Rouault**,
Bathing in a Lake, 1907.
Pastel and watercolour on paper,
65 x 96 cm.
Pushkin State Museum of Fine Arts, Moscow.

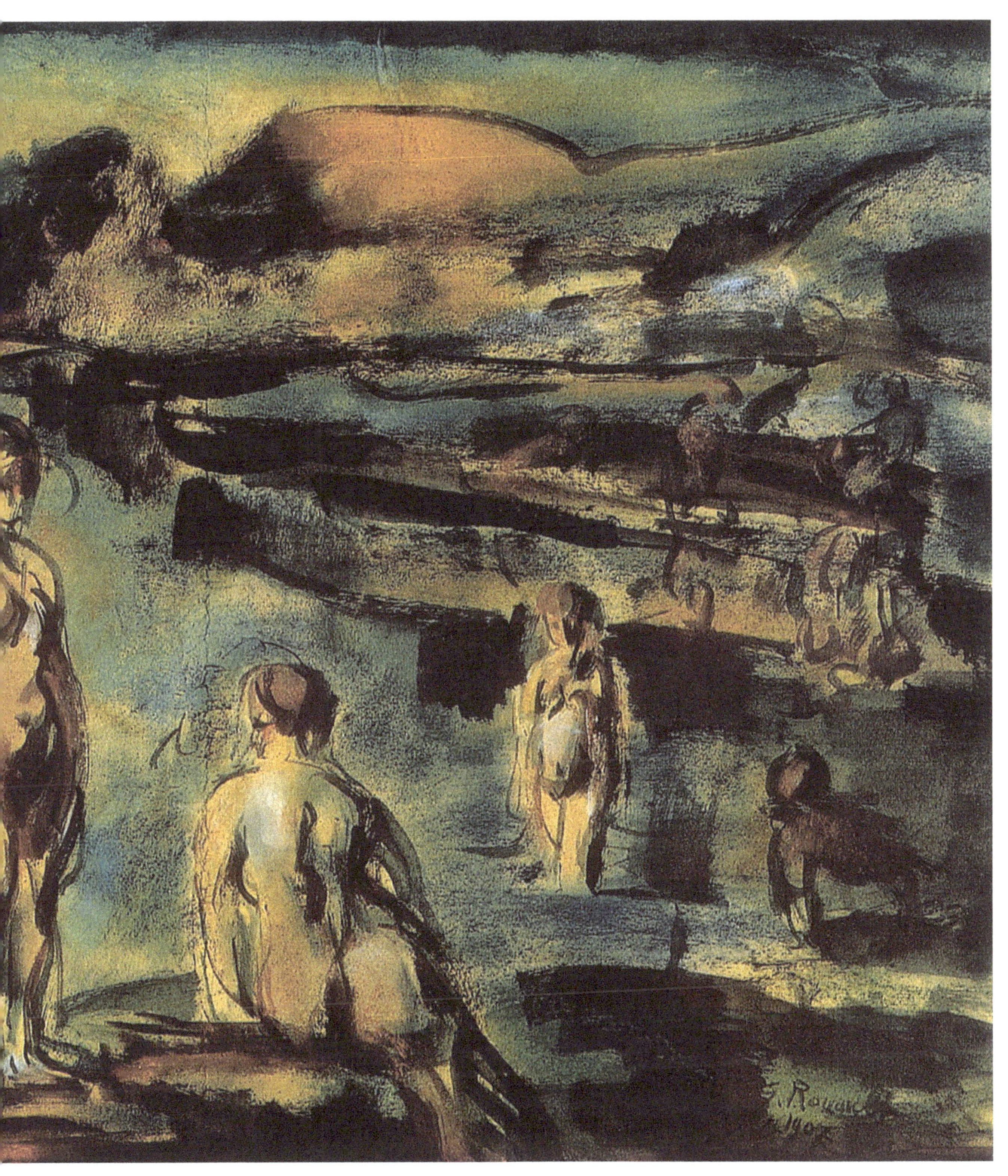

the founders of the 'Salon d'Automne ', in 1905 he was with his friends under the banner of "Matisse's group" at the 'Salon des Indépendants 'and, finally, at the celebrated 1905 'Salon d'Automne' he was one of those christened "Fauves."

Outwardly Rouault's life was just as ordinary. It was spent for the most part in Paris. In 1910 the Galerie Druet organized Rouault's first personal exhibition – 183 works, comprising paintings, drawings, and ceramics. Later the artist fulfilled many commissions for Vollard. From the beginning of the 1930s Rouault exhibitions were arranged all over the globe, including America. The artist's eightieth birthday was marked by huge retrospectives in Paris, Brussels, Amsterdam, New York, Tokyo, and Milan.

Rouault's painting rarely went beyond the usual Fauvist genres – landscape and still life, and was restricted to a range of themes already established in his youth – clowns, prostitutes, court officials, and the Passion of Christ. Yet the continual repetition of the same set of subjects in his painting over a period of seventy years has not rendered it monotonous; on the contrary, it demands a special kind of concentration far removed from the shock or simple quick reaction most often evoked by the works of his friends.

Between 1903 and 1914 Rouault produced variations on the theme, each new drawing or painting revealed some new nuance in this seemingly unchanging world. In *Les Filles (The girls)*, he is rather turning things over in his mind, making the viewer a fellow-witness of the figures frozen before him which possess both an expressive ugliness and, at the same time, an attractive openness.

Bathing in a Lake was produced in the same period and in the same key as regards colour and form. With *Spring* (1911, Hermitage) the rose window of a Gothic cathedral simply leaps into the mind. Lines diverge from the centre, broad, soft contours dividing the circle into separate parts. Warm colours – a dull red and gold – are present only in a few sparse outcrops; the petals of the rose are filled with a pale blue which glows like the glass in a leaded window. The beauty of *Spring* is founded entirely on rhythm and colour.

In Rouault's work, the boundary between graphic art and painting is not a clearly defined one – his graphic pieces, even the black and white ones, are always picturesque; his painted sheets – produced in a combination of tempera, gouache, watercolour and pastel – are often taken for graphic works. Rouault's work goes beyond the generally accepted conceptions which hold Fauvism to have been limited to researching expressive form.

Shortly before dying, Rouault destroyed about 300 of his pictures, simply because he felt that he would not live long enough to finish them. Rouault died in Paris in 1958

▶ **Georges Rouault,** 1871-1958, Expressionism, French, *The Holy Face (Christ)*, 1933. Oil and gouache on paper mounted on canvas, 91 x 65 cm. Musée national d'art moderne, Centre Georges-Pompidou, Paris..

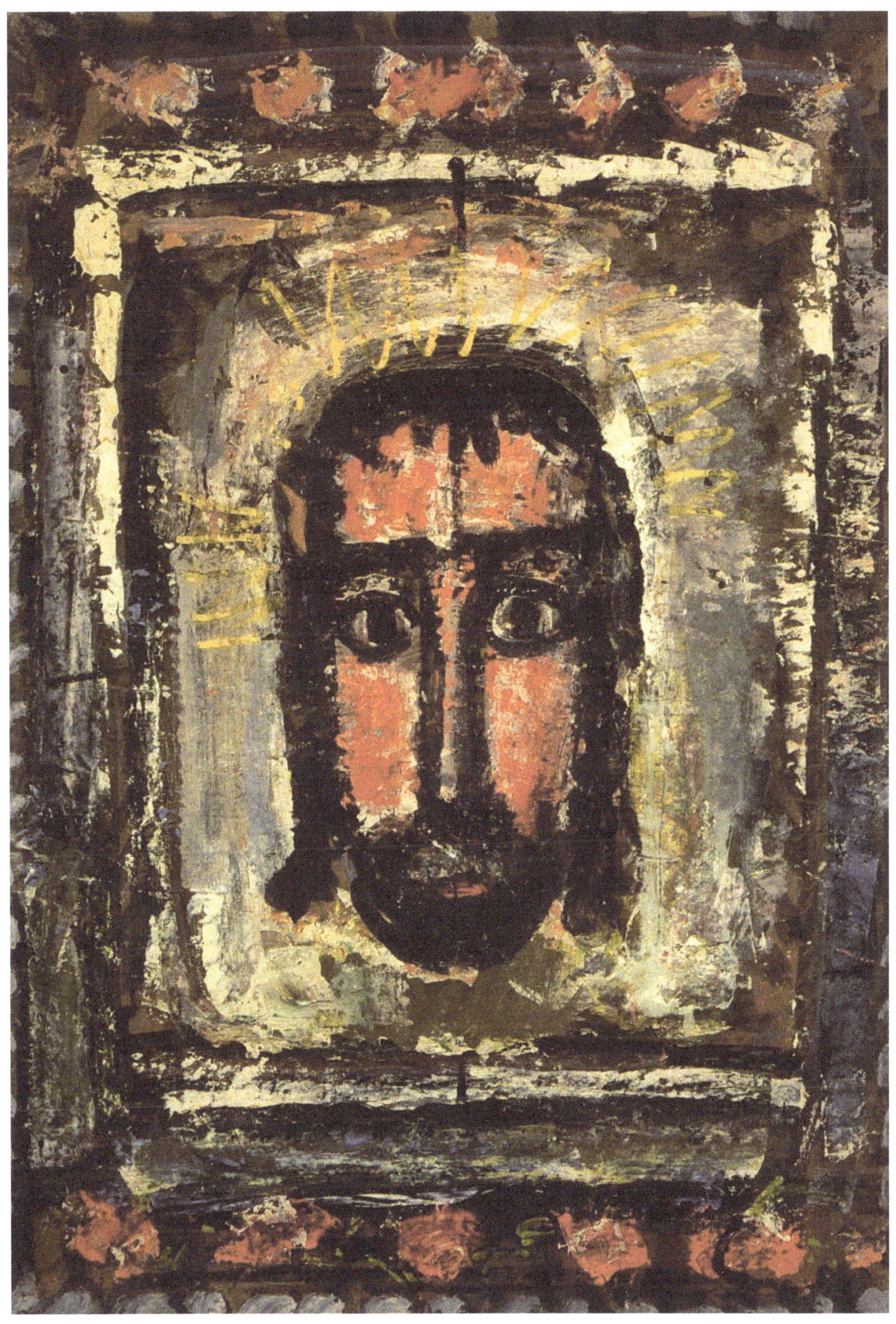

LIST OF ILLUSTRATIONS

V de Vlaminck, Maurice

ART HISTORY COLLECTION

- Abstract Art
- Art Deco
- Art Nouveau
- Baroque
- Byzantine Art
- Chinese Art
- Cubism
- Dada
- Early Italian Art
- Egypt Art
- Expressionism
- Gothic Art
- Greek Art
- Impressionism
- Indian Art
- Naive Art
- Neoclassicism
- Persian Art
- Post-Impressionism
- Realism
- Renaissance
- Pre-Raphaelites
- Rococo
- Roman Art
- Romanesque Art
- Romanticism
- Surrealism
- Symbolism
- The Fauves
- The Viennese Secession

www.ingramcontent.com/pod-product-compliance
Lightning Source LLC
Chambersburg PA
CBHW040855070726
47689CB00056B/86
9781683259404